BOAT RACING

Now and Then

Ralph DeSilva

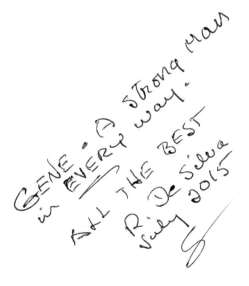

GENE - A strong man in EVERY way. ALL THE BEST R. DeSilva July 2015

Publication: 2015 —1st Edition Print

For information on this book, write:

Ralph DeSilva
P.O. Box 1296
Hiram GA, 30141

Cover and Photo Credit from Powerboat, June 1970 Issue, Photo by Roger Squire

Dedication

To Norm and Ann: Two incredible miracles.

*****

I am indebted to those who have read, advised and edited this manuscript, and those who have given counsel on historical matters.

This work is one-sided, my viewpoint. Ten people can observe an event, any scene, and there will be ten different versions of it. I apologize for any errors of memory. On the whole, I believe, this book is accurate.

I especially want to dedicate this book to all those who have spent time in the cockpit of a race boat— Inboard, Outboard, Tunnel, hydroplane or runabout. It is those folks, those who have experienced the relationship of boat at high speed and its reaction to the water, who know and understand this unique sensation.

All the elements of nature are involved, gravity, the laws of Newton and Bernoulli, and almost everything else we learned in Physics, come into play in boat racing.

Stinson Drives Outboard to Win

Parker, Ariz—Allan Stinson of Pittsburgh became the first outboard driver ever to win the Parker 9-Hour Enduro as he drove his DeSilva Hull craft to a record-chattering win here Sunday before an estimated 35,000 fans.

Bobby Massey of Paramount suffered a broken arm when he was thrown from his boat, He was flown to Palm Springs for treatment.

1.Allan Stinson (Pittsburgh), DeSilva Hill, $2,000; 2. Ron Hill (Garden Grove), Hallet Hydro, $1,000; 3. Robert Whitt (Baytown Tex), Glaston-Monilari, $750; 4. Allan Yaw (Abilerie, Tex.), Molinari, $450; 5. Jim McConnell (Victorville) DeSilva Hull, $230; 6. Bob Hammond (Austin, Tex.), Molinari, $150; 7. Ted May (Long Beach), OMC Hydro, $125; 8. Bill Seebold (Fondulac, Wis), Ron Jones Hull, $100; 9. Waiter Hower (Burlingame), Aqua-craft, $75; 10. H.T. McCune (Denver), Schulze Hydro $50.

[The following was written by Claude Fox for publication in the NOA newsletter, "Roostertale," in the early '50's]

A Short History.

1946 Los Angeles

This was one of the first boats built by the brothers after resuming construction after WWII. The boat was not intended for racing, the customer wanted a fast boat to be used on the Colorado River. The boat was 10'6" long and 52" wide to be powered by a 15 HP Evinrude pleasure motor.

The boat was a trendsetter but not without flaws. It was not a good rough water boat and even at the low attained speed of 35 mph had a tendency to oscillate.

This boat was the first of the banana boat series, which lasted until 1954.

When the stock racing category arrived in 1947 it was relatively easy to modify some designs to make a competitive boat. The stock program required a double-cockpit, conservative design in contrast to the then current Alky race boat.

Boat racing as we know it began in the mid-1920's. Local boat clubs, with the introduction of efficient, low weight Outboard Motors, began to conduct races for the membership.

Boats at that time were open or double cockpit runabouts—on step up from a row boat. Races were usually marathons or point-to-point. Circle races then became popular, usually with a flag boat for the starts. The Delta region of Northern California was a natural venue for this new and exciting sport. Boats of this early period were built by traditional, old line boat builders, using their familiar materials and craftsmanship. Early on there were no rules and regulations.

There was one boat name, it started in 1926, which is still active today. That company is DeSilva, of Georgia. In the mid-1920's John DeSilva was a building contractor in Pittsburgh, California. At the time U.S. Steel had just constructed a great new steel mill in Pittsburgh and the rapid growth stimulated by the mill created a good business climate for John.

To keep pace with some friends he purchased a new, four-cylinder Caille outboard motor and, using his woodworking skill and design talent, built a boat. The hull turned out very well and favorably impressed the local boating group. The boat, when completed, was named Billy Boy after John's second son. John's boat created a good bit if interest and he soon began to spend part of his time building boats for others who wanted a sample of his lighter weight product with its fine craftsmanship. The 1929 Stock Market crash and subsequent depression adversely affected the contracting business. The public seemed unable to purchase new homes or other big ticket consumer goods, but a good many did seem able to spend money in the new sport of boat racing. As a result, John started the DeSilva Boat Company and began to devote all of his time to the design and construction of racing boats.

Boat speed in the latter part of the 1920's was sufficient to make a hydroplane preform efficiently. The impetus of the hydro gave a big boost to the growth of boat racing. The hydroplane started as a long, slender hull with side sponsons, then evolved into the very successful single-step design. The West Coast continued to be very strong runabout country. Builders such as Rockholt, Collins, Phantom, Zimmerman and Cowden were prominent and could be seen at all the regattas. It was not unusual to have twenty to thirty runabouts entered in any one of the three runabout outboard classes. In addition to the DeSilva hydro, evident at the local races were Elsinor, Jocoby, Flowers and a few others.

1987   Knoxville Tennessee

Left to right: Claude Fox, Art Pugh (Far right)

It is doubtful anyone will be able to detail fox's contribution to outboard racing in the US. He was responsible for the rebirth of the NOA in 1951 and enabled that organization to help build outboard racing into a force that made boat racing America the envy of the boat world.

Art Pugh is the patriarch of a boat racing clan. His son, Gary, is now a major builder of fine race boats.

By 1932 a DeSilva boat had established a national record—that of Martin Leach of Modesto, California, who set a C service Runabout competition record of 37.34 mph. Through World War Two the demand for the DeSilva boat was sufficient such that the boats were primarily sold on the West Coast. During the war things were static, and John devoted himself to building small, lapstrake dories for the Navy.

After the war John's two sons, Ralph and Bill, returned from Service and took over the boat business. At that time there was sufficient strength in boat racing to keep the boys busy building for the California market. As time went on the West Coast became the market—and then the nation. Some outboard racing activity with Stock, Pleasure, or Fishing motors began after WWII. Sectioning associations such as the NOA and the APBA recognized the potential created by the Mercury Outboard motor company, and a formal Stock Racing program began in the U.S. The category grew beyond everyone's expectations and created a great new market for the brothers. During this period the Alky Division had suffered because new motors were not readily available. Prior to the war Johnson had made the Pr-65 and the P-50 service motors. Evinrude had been the manufacturer of the 6042 Hex Head C motor, the Midget M, and the Speedi-twin C Service motor. The amalgamated OMC Co, dropped these racing motors during the way and never resumed their construction. Parts and pieces were available from the aftermarket— from such as Hubble, Wiseman, Fuller, Jones, Vincent, and a few others. They kept the Alky Division going, but this situation did not lend itself to a needed growth.

1949

Fifteen year old Robert parish has just won class A runabout at the Colorado River Marathon

The Stock program provided easy entry into boat racing because new motors and parts were available through local boat and motor dealers. At inception, the Stock program consisted of three classes: A, B and C runabout. The D class was added with a short time. The Stock program started just as the Alky Division twenty years previously. Because the runabout has always been the DeSilva forte, their boats quickly set design and performance standards. Several years into the program, hydroplanes were added into the Stock program.

In the 1950's the sport of Drag racing, both Inboard and Outboard, began in Southern California and again the DeSilva boat was there. In 1958 one of their inboard hydros, the Witch, went through the lights at the then unbelievable speed of 160+ mph. Over the years, DeSilva products have been used by virtually every prominent boat racer in the Alky and Stock divisions: the list of names would be in the Who's who of boat racing.

1954 was a typical year for DeSilva boats. Bobby Parish, a Bakersfield, CA schoolboy, won the A Stock hydro National Championship in De Pere, WI, and at the same regatta placed second in the B

8

Runabout. At the same Nationals, Ron Loomis of Santa Barbara, CA won the C Stock Runabout. (Twenty-nine years later, Dave Bryan of Hemet, CA repeated the feat by winning in the APBA Nationals in the same class. In 1958 Dave had begun the effort to win the Nationals and for Twenty-Four years raced his own homebuilt runabout. In 1982 he bought a DeSilva and won the Nationals in 1983.) Also in 1954 Louis Meyer, Jr ("Sonny") of Indy Meyer/Drake Offenhauser fame established a 48 CID hydro competition record, at Salton Sea, of 61.76 mph. DeSilva runabouts won championships in NOA and APBA Alky Classes that year.

Numerous times DeSilva runabouts have won all the championships in both NOA and APBA Regattas. In some years their hydros have also won, as in 1958 in Springfield, IL, where in addition to all the runabout championships they also won the NOA B Hydro (Dale Kaus/Anzani). In 1960 Bill Tenney repeated the win with Dick Pond, at the NOA championships in St. Paul.

At About the same time Drag Racing was getting underway, the OPC program got its start—again in California. Two giant Marathons, the Havasu Two-Day Classic and the Parker Nine Hour, set the stage for a national program. A twenty-foot DeSilva twin engine Wing 4pt. design won the 1970 Parker Marathon, on the Colorado River, and set a course record of 81+ mph for the nine hours (Alan Stinson/Jerry Walin). A second Wing Also placed 5th (McConnel/Zorkin). This was the first time that the Outboards were also to best the might inboards powered by huge automotive engines. Earlier, in 1966, a unique eighteen foot twin engine runabout was designed by the DeSilva for OMC to run in the Havasu Marathon. Driven by Fred Hausenstein, the boat did not win, but it was the prototype for what is now known as the Mod VP design. Ron Hill, of Bellflower, CA, later drove the boat to many victories in the California COBRA circuit.

DeSilva boats have frequently won every Runabout class at the Alky National Championships, and occasionally have held every Kilo and Competition record for Alky Runabouts. While they emphasized Alky runabouts, boats for other divisions have, over the years, won Championships and held the records.

Because boat racing demands the utmost in craft strength and performance, standard boat hardware was not suitable. It was necessary to make custom pieces designed for a specific purpose. For years, the DeSilva Boat Co. made hardware only for their own boats. Then, gradually, a few items were sold commercially. The hardware line was then expanded and made available to the boating public. Now, the company provides the most comprehensive line of high performance and racing hardware in the U.S.

BOAT RACING - THEN AND NOW
******

The DeSilva shop moved from Northern California to the Atlanta, Georgia area in 1981 because an increasing amount of business came from out of California and Common Carriers had placed a prohibitive freight rate on boats—especially racing boats with their bulk and lightweight. Whereas a good many boats had been shipped via Air Freight, most all Carriers had gone to a container mode, which eliminated boats. The Georgia location has proven to be a good one, as it is readily accessible from the major boat racing areas east of Mississippi.

Dave Berg, Minneapolis, Minnesota, schoolboy enters a turn with his Anzani class A Alky powered flat deck runabout.

Dave was a formidable competitor among a group of young men who started boat racing after WWII. The Michigan, Minnesota, Wisconsin, Illinois area of the mid-west became a hotbed for drivers who became boat racing legends.

Photo-Koopman,1958

1955 oil city Louisiana

Left to Right: Dave Barnes, Zanesville, OH (World champion in class C-1 Hydroplane), Bob McGinty, Corpus Christia, Tx (World champion in Class C Racing Runabout), Deanie Montgomery, Corsicana, TX (World Champion in Class A Hydroplane), Homer Kincaid, Carbon Cliff, IL (Winner Class B National High-Point and the "Jack Lockheart Memorial Trophy"(Pictured in front of him). Jim Griffen, Quicy, IL (World champion in Class F Hydroplane, Bill Seebold, Granite City, IL (World Champion in Class C Hydroplane), Ellis Willoughby, Alexander IL (World Champion in Class C-1 runabout). Kneeling Deiter Konig, Berlin, Germany with the Sportsman Trophy and Clay Petterrer and Lake Charles Louisisana with the Tatum Trophy for free for all runabout.

A boat race always results in a few happy winners. Here are a few who came south and are going north with a championship. Bob McGinty will travel only a few miles west of Shrevenport, where he will show his trophy to Harry Marioneaux; his equipment owner.

Homer Kincaid, Caron Cliff, Illinois, mechanical engineer, receives only one of many past and future accomplishments. Few will ever attain his stature in Alky outboard racing. Dieter Konig, Berlin, Germany, has come to America to promote his outboard racing motors. He has also proven to be a good boat driver.

Bernie Van Osdale

DeSilva racing boats, the most recognized name in boat racing, is the story of a father and two sons who started building fast, little boats in the late 1920's in Southern California. My first knowledge of DeSilva boats was through their advertisements in *Boat Sport and Speed &Spray* magazines in the 1950's. As a kid then, little did I know that when I grew up I would race their boats and become good friends.

I do not remember exactly when I first met Bill and Ralph. It was probably at my first APBA Nationals in Winona in 1976. I do remember that each year I would see them walking around the pits greeting old friends and making new ones. Both brothers would stop and help any driver that had particular concern about how his boat might be handling. Ralph, who has not changed in appearance since I first met him always wearing his small carpenter apron with a tape measure and pencil in it. Bill would quietly listen and offer a few suggestions. I remember both Bill and Ralph standing in different locations, each with binoculars, watching how their boats were preforming on the water. Neither one ever said much, but one combined their observations into the next improvement of the racing boats. I always felt that Ralph was the designer and that Bill was the artist that turned the boats into masterpieces. But in reality, they were a team that completed each other. Together they gave outboard boat racers the thrill of their lives.

I have owned and raced five different DeSilva runabouts over my thirty-five year racing career. The first, a big old heavy 13' foot boat built in the late 1950's that had an aluminum plate in the bottom. The

Marshall Grant (in cockpit), owner of the "Ring Of Fire", poses with Cash (on deck) and other members of the Cash band.

idea was that the aluminum would keep the bottom straight. It didn't work. Although the plate didn't warp, the bottom stringers did.

My second DeSilva was the Ring of Fire II, built for Marshall Grant and raced famously by Dickie Pond and Billy Seebold. Bill and Ralph started building boats for Marshal Grant in 1961. They built seven runabouts from 1961 to 1974.

Only three of these boats carried the name Ring of Fire. The first of these was built in 1963 and is the one picture on the cover of *Boat Racing* magazine with Johnny Cash sitting on the deck. DeSilva built two more runabouts that bore the names Ring of Fire II (1967), and Ring of Fire Jr. (969). Ring of Fire II was a 13' CD Runabout and Jr. was a 13' B runabout. The whereabouts of the Ring of Fire and Ring of Fire Jr. is unknown.

BOAT RACING - THEN AND NOW

I bought the boat from Duke Johnson in the fall of 1977 and raced it until 1998. Duke got Ring of Fire II from Grant in 1971 after the annual Alexandria, LA regatta. Since Duke helped Grant a lot at the races, Marshall gave him the boat for the price of the hardware ($200). That is the same deal Duke gave me. Since I didn't have any money at the time, my girlfriend, now wife, Cindy, paid for it. I guess the boat is really hers since I never paid her back. This was the boat that I drove to two Canadian National Championships in C-Service Runabout in 1978 and 1979. I continued banging around race courses for years with this old war horse getting a few seconds and thirds at De Pue in C-Service and C-Race in the 1990's. For those who know me, the original Rung of Fire II is the repainted orange M-12.

During the 80's and 90's, I occasionally raced two other DeSilva's that I had acquired in various deals that I made in order to get a few Evinrudes that I wanted. The first, a 1970 boat that was one of the bright red runabouts named Frustration raced by Jerry Simison. The boat had a 27" bottom, which also made it prone to taking flight. It was also the boat that Bob Rake was driving in the infamous seven boat pile-up in Alexandria, La, in 1976. Wayne Baldwin has a series of photos that shows the accident in progression. I heard, but can't confirm, that his pile up was so impressive that it made ABC's *Wide World of Sports*. I won the 1985 Evinrude-only Nationals and the 1989 PR Runabout Nationals at De Pue, with this boat. The other was a 1977 KR DeSilva. The KR was a new design runabout that Bill and Ralph introduced in 1974 that was an improvement over the older, flat deck style boat. I never liked this boat much because it would sometimes turn end for end in the corner. If a driver would drive outside on the turns, keeping the RPM's up and the bow up, there would be no problems. This boat is still active with driver Steve Bolhuis consistently finishing in the top three positions at the stock Top-of-Michigan marathon races. It is a great rough water boat for C-Stock.

My last and favorite boat is a C-Service/C-racing Runabout that Bill and Ralph DeSilva built specially for Wes Jones in 1996. Jones, the famous manufacturer of cylinders for Johnson PR's, never lost his love for the old iron racing engines. Late in his life, he got back into boat racing and teamed up with the DeSilva brothers. The boat that Bill and Ralph built for him is, to my mind, the most beautiful boat that they ever built. I bought this boat in 1999. The boat is really a piece of art. The boat won the APBA Nationals in C-Service Runabout in 1997 with Loren Waters driving.

I still have three of the five runabouts that I raced for so many years. I will never forget the many triumphs and screw-ups that happened to me at the different race courses around the mid-west. I will never forget the friendships that I have made with many boat racers, and I will especially remember and cherish my friendships with Bill and Ralph.

*****

Marathon Outboard racing was big at the turn of the century. Top of Michigan was one of the bigger events – Bill Groggin was a dedicated devotee.

22M was built specifically for marathon racing – the boat had added structural strength and was designed to cope with adverse water conditions – at speed.

Bill purchased an unfinished boat – he wanted an absolutely first class trim and finish, so he managed finish himself. He achieved his goal – the photo is proof.

Photo-Groggin

Run—Run for Cover!

It started with a phone call from Pep Hubbell in 1958; He had just had an experience on his dynamometer. Over a period of time, he had checked many motors on his dyno—large and small, efficient outboard racing motors.

Occasionally he had worked on the largest outboard pleasure motors, putting them on the tester and checking the factory horsepower ratings. His attitude was: don't tell me; I'll prove the point.

Anyway, a motor on his dyno had just produced the largest horsepower ever. It was a 4 cylinder Mercury 44CID, with a megaphone exhaust.

Pep was astounding. A Mercury! A brand noted as a Stock racing motor showing more horsepower than the largest of the Alky racing motors. How could this be?

Mercury motors, of course, had been modified and raced with the various Alky classes for several years, with only moderate success.

We had sold boats to a company in Quincy, Illinois, which had begun to campaign their modified Mercury motors, and were claiming great hose power and speed. One of the Quincy drivers, Fred Goehl, had recently set an NOA Alky kilo B runabout record of 60+mph. This was not to be taken lightly. Sixty mph had long been the speed target of most Alky classes!

And to have a Mercury motor of 20 CID do it on a runabout was truly amazing.

O.F. Christner, head of the Quincy organization, was confident that his Mercury modified motors would soon prove their worth. This proved to be quite true. For over a generation, the Quincy group equipment raced against the world's best and proved that the brand was second to none.

A short time later after Hubbell's phone conversation, a fellow walked into the shop. He had been advised that we had a large new hydro and asked if it was available for some testing.

Aside from his introducing himself as Marshall Grant, we knew nothing about the man. He looked around 30-35 and appeared physically fit. We were told that he was a member of the Tennessee Three and the Johnny Cash group.

We loaned Mr. Grant a hydro which he was to test at an upcoming race at Long Beach Marine Stadium—our decision was especially easy after learning that he was the owner of the motor that Hubbell had Dyno Tested.

We helped Grant setup for the short Sunday morning test session. The crowd was usual, cars were parked on both sides of the canal, with many spectators at the water's edge playing or wading.

Marshal probably did create the Tennessee three. It was a Memphis neighborhood thing. He learned the play guitar at an early age and found a kid who liked drums. They ran across an older fellow who was good enough to play lead guitar.

They got together and performed at social events and public functions. Marshal made his living as a mechanic at a local auto dealership.

They became pretty good, but needed a front man who looked OK and could sing a bit. They ran across a fellow who was trying to get established in the music business. He was named John Cash. He didn't have a great voice but he had something-and he looked OK.

Within a few years they had developed a sound. It wasn't Glenn Miller but it was pretty good. Marshal had switched from a guitar to a base guitar. Because they had a good lead guitar, Marshal stated learning to play the base for theme and volume. In doing so, he developed their theme sound and it brought them fame and fortune. The rest is history-and you know the story.

Marshal Grant's boat racing team began sometime in the late '50's. He became friends with an old time boat racer named PG Sweet. They fooled around with some local racing around Memphis.

Marshal moved his family to North Hollywood because John Cash became involved as an actor-they used Southern California as a headquarters. They performed all over the USA-all over the world. Whenever possible Marshal worked on his boat racing equipment and attended boat races.

His occupational contract did not allow him to drive-he, at various times, used such drivers as Dick Pond, Bill Seebold Jr. and a few others of that talent.

Marshall cranked the motor and stroked slowly down the channel to the Eastern 2nd buoy, then turned and applied throttle as he came into the straightaway. The motor came to life with the full roar of the megaphone exhaust pipes.

No one had ever heard such racket out of an outboard motor or seen a boat hurtle down the straight at such speed. Women ran to the water, grabbed their kids' hands and headed for their cars. This had to be something bad!

1969 Alexandria, LA

Grant ran around the course several times, with the full attention of the other drivers and the spectators. He returned to the pits, said the motor was running okay and thanked us for the boat loan.

We were told that his contract did not allow him to drive a race boat due to the hazards of racing, but that he intended to campaign with other drivers.

Sometime later he sold his home in the San

Left to right: Arlen Crouch, Marshal Grant.

A tete a tete at the NOW Nationals. Arlen was a member of the original Quincy Welding drive team of Fred Goehl, Arlen Crouch, David Christner and Gene East. Crouch and Goehl tended to drive the larger, more powerful motors, while Christner and East were pilots of small motors.

In 1955, Goehl drove a Mercury powered B Alky runabout to a Kilo record in excess of 60mph. This was astounding because it was not till after WWII that a PR Johnson was able to attain a speed of 60mph on a runabout and that was not till 1952-53.

Arlen was especially noted for the ability to put the Quincy D and F equipment up front at the big important regattas.

Fernando Valley and returned to Memphis. Thereafter he had a pick of outstanding drivers, such as Dick Pond, Bill Seebold and others who placed the Marshal Grant equipment at the top of Outboard Alky boat racing for over a generation.

One can safely say that Marshall Grand introduced the Mercury Alky motor into the West Coast with his performance at a minor boat race in Long Beach, 1958.

1963 Knoxville Tennessee

John Cash often joined co-worker Marhsal grant at boat racing events, as often as their hectic music career allowed.
Cash was not a boat race participant, he was an interest spectator. Marshal was the lead member of the Tennessee three and the other members o the group took his hobby very seriously.
A time or two the whole entourage performed at a regatta in order to enhance public attendance.
The man in black, in 1963, had attained a premier status in country music and his presence guaranteed a very big turnout

Photo-Rome

Left to right: Fred Brinkman, Springfield, IL, Robert Murphy, Springfield, IL, James Geary, Minnesota

Fred Brinkman had just sold his C service runabout V88 and motor to Murphy, who was to win over a period of many years, a number of championships and records in both the NOA and APBA.

Jim Geary, an outboard race enthusiast, was a pitman extraordinaire.
1969 DePue Illinois

19

RITTEN & EDITED BY SUSAN, DOROTHY & RICHARD JOY

THE BARNSTORMERS WIN!

The Barnstormer Racing Team won a 3 heat clean sweep victory in the Antique C Service Hydro Class at the DePue Nationals.

Wes Jones of Wilmington, Delaware had brought his DeSilva built boats and his Jones PR Motors to DePue for the races. Wes is a master engine builder and a former race driver.

Veteran race boat driver Matt Dagastino of Bowie, Maryland came with Wes to drive the boats for the Barnstormer Racing Team.

Ralph DeSilva, the builder of Wes' boats came up from Hiram, Georgia to set up the new runabout he had built for Wes and to help with setting up the teams other DeSilva Boats.

Guy and Richard Joy of Keithsburg, Illinois had planned on bringing their Joy Speeditwin Motor for Jack Campbell to race on his boat. Unfortunately, Jack had some medical problems and was unable to attend. The Joy's decided to go ahead and come to DePue hoping someone else might race the motor. When they got to the races the Barnstormers agreed to use the Joy Speeditwin on their boats in the service classes.

The winning combination which also included a prop provided by Karl Williams, was put together right there at the races. To win a championship at the Nationals with an untested combination put together at the race is, in the words of Master Boat Builder Ralph DeSilva, "A Minor Miracle".

With the help of the Barnstormers pit crew consisting of Henry Cotterill of Milford, PA, Dustin Joy of Illinois City, IL, and Richard Joy and the expert driving skills of Matt Dagastino the Barnstormers also posted second place victories in ACSR, ACRR, and ACRH.

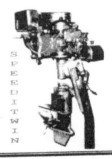

S
P
E
E
D
I
T
W
I
N

First Time

Often I've been asked, "When was your first boat race?"

Ok, the year was 1929. A boat race—a marathon— was to take place between Antioch and Stockton. Antioch is on the San Joaquin River, east of Pittsburgh near the entrance to the Sacramento River, on the channel to Stockton. As the crow flies, it is about twenty miles, but on the meandering river, the distance is more than forty.

The very first races in California were marathons. This was before closed course sanctioned races arrived. Local clubs within the Delta would sponsor an event between a site or community. Participants would sign up for the event, a signal or patrol boat would line up all the boats through flag signals, then wave the fleet on its way.

Boat race drivers and family posing in front of the boathouse at the Olympic Marine Stadium.
Left to Right: Unknown couple, Mr. & Mrs. Andrew Laird, Tracy, CA, Ernie Millot, Stockton, CA, Mrs. Cliff Ruhland, Marysville, CA.
Kneeling: Rodney Pantages, Hollywood, CA, Chester Livingston, Stockton, CA

BOAT RACING - THEN AND NOW

There were about twenty or more boats on the water and I found myself in the cockpit of a runabout my father had built for Ernie Millot. I was to be his deck rider. A deck rider is supposed to throw himself on the flat deck as the boat enters a turn. Then, assuming all is well, return to the cockpit rear.

I don't quite remember the circumstances as to how and why I found myself on that vast expanse of water, on what seemed to be the most unstable thing I had ever imagined. The boats circled around in what seemed a random mad-house, without reason, until a large boat with four or five persons began waving flags.

All the boats then proceed in one direction up the river. After what seemed a very long time, but probably not much more than five minutes, we were alone and in the lead. There was only the roar of the two cylinder motor and Ernie calmly piloting us on our way.

The river was a maze of passageways with no sign pointing to Stockton. I really hoped Ernie was going in the right direction because I had no idea where we were. Mostly we were on a water level several feet above farm land on each side.

Once we passed a huge ocean freighter gliding along. It produced very little wake and we motored by as several crew members waved high above us.

I became very thirsty—probably because my mouth had been open much of the time. I had to blink a good eal because of the wind velocity. I was doing alright: Ernie had made no complaint.

I was really beginning to tire when the great Stockton commercial warehouse district appeared on the right, alongside the ship turning basic. Soon we saw McCleod's Lake and Steamboat Levee, on which Millot's floating boat shop and marina was located. We were first to arrive—we had won!

It took me several moments to find a normal equilibrium, but I was delighted to get out of the boat, onto something firm. Ernie had a soft drink cabinet and asked what flavor I liked. "Root Beer," I answered.

I still like Root beer, but sadly the Nehi brand is no more.

Ernie Millot

It was inevitable that in the extensive boating in California that a good many wanted to go faster and perhaps prove that their equipment may be proven faster. There was only one way to do that-through some form of competition.

The very first races in California were marathons. This was before the closed course arrived. Local clubs in the Delta would sponsor an event between a site or community. Participants would sign up for the event, a signal or patrol boat would line all the boats through flag signals, then wave the fleet on its way.

You can be sure that Ernie Millott went home a happy man after his win of the C Runabout class at the Hearst Regatta.

They do not give such epic trophies today, but this was a William Randolph Hearst newspaper event – a giant perpetual trophy and a handsomely decorated radio were not big thing for such a happening.

Ernie later retired the large trophy; which is sometimes awarded to some outstanding driving event or accomplishment by a current northern California boat race driver.

One such event I vividly remember. It was 1928-29 – a marathon between Antioch and Stockton, on the Sacramento, then into the San Joaquin rivers.

My father volunteered me to ride as mechanic with Ernie Millot, on a new runabout he had just built. I had been aboard my father's runabout many times of course, but not in a marathon regatta. Ernie's boat was a double cockpit model. I found myself alongside Ernie in the Rear cockpit, with no handles to grab. My death grip on Ernie's boat somewhat relaxed after the flag boat waved a fair start and we found ourselves in the lead on a tributary off the main channel.

It took about 45 minutes to navigate the sloughs, channels and creek to the final destination – Millott's boat house landing on McCleod's lake, downtown Stockton.

Ernie had started occupation as an auto mechanic in Stockton. In the mid 20's he began working for the leading Stockton outboard dealer. Prior to my 1st boat race adventure, he had taken over a big floating covered boat house landing. He had a machine shop, living quarters and petrol sales setup and soft drink outlet. This was during the Prohibition Era. Ernie didn't sell liquor, but I can remember plenty of drinking alcohol at these festive local events.

McCleod's Lake was a stone's throw from the Stockton City Hall and major downtown faculties. Last time I was in Stockton (1960's) the lake had been filled in and all the great boat houses on the lake were gone.

While there were a good number of notable personalities prominent in California during the late 20's and early 30's no one was more active and influential than Ernie Millott.

My father was fortunate to live within Millott's orbit in Northern California, for Ernie seemed to have an extraordinary ability to extract extra horsepower from an outboard motor. Most drivers of the day at one time or another had Millott work on their equipment. He also made himself a fine driver of both the runabout and hydroplane.

It must be remembered that, in Northern California, the hydroplane did not arrive in viable quantity until 1930.

Of all the motors that Ernie worked on, he expressed special affection for the 22 HP Evinrude Service and motor and the Johnson PR65. The Evinrude was 1st designed in the late 20's and became extremely popular after introduction. The PR65 arrived in 1934. I can remember Millott working his small shop, over the water, in Stockton while he put together a motor for some impending race. He was fortunate in being able to make a living work on what he loved to do. Ernie Millott married Mezzie sometime in the early 30's. Mezzie was a Stockton divorcee, with two young daughters, who had been seriously bitten with the outboard bug. After marriage they became a formidable racing team – both driving multiple classes and most often dominating wherever they went. They raced all over the US and especially up and down the west coast. Ernie Millot was killed while driving an F racing 2 man runabout at Lakeport, California, during a regatta in 1940.

Uruguay 1990

This is proof that boat racing is not restricted to the US, Europe and Australia.

A Mr. Daniel Carsarino contacted us in 1989 about a small runabout to be driven in the South American country. Powered by a stock commercial outboard motor, their sport is the source of pleasure for the driver and spectators.

Situated near altitude 40 – about in line with Sidney, Australia, the climate is conductive to great water sports.

Rules and Regulations: The Early Days

Because inboard boat racing was a flourishing sport prior to World War I, the infant governing organization, the American Powerboat Organization (APBA), organized in 1903, had boat racing well in hand. After 1920, increasingly large numbers of outboards were sold to the general population. The larger horsepower motors naturally provided some speed—and speed required competition.

Local outboard clubs sprang up all over the US. It can safely be said that outboard racing originated as a local neighborhood sport. As the sport mushroomed and became more professional, the need for rules and regulation became absolutely essential. In 1924, the APBA formulated a set of rules for outboard racing.

Classes were established through piston displacement as in most other motorized competition racing. The first classes:

Class A	12 or under CID
Class B	12 to 17 CID
Class C	17 to 30 CID
Class D	over 30 CID

In 1927, the classes were reorganized to conform to motors then available. The APBA setup and outboard committee which changed the classes:

Class A	Under 15 CID
Class B	15-20 CID
Class C	20-30 CID
Class D	30-40 CID
Class E	40-50 CID

In 1930, Class F was created to provide for the newly introduced OMC 60 CID motor. Class X was also created for motors over 60 CID or those who wanted to run a non-stock motor.

Evinrude, in 1931, offered the M racing motor. This was to be a class for the novice, an inexperienced, slower speed class. In 1933 the class M was off probation and an established class for hydroplanes.

1943 F Runabout

This semi-completed runabout is an example of the John DeSilva workmanship. The boat was built as inventory during WWII; and was sold to Hovey Cook, Covina, California, who campaigned the boat very successfully till it was destroyed through a trailer fire while enroute to a boat race in 1953.

The APBA divided racing into two categories, amateur and professional. Early on, the APBA recognized that some provision must be made for those who wanted to remain amateur and compete in AAU (Amateur Athletic Union) sports or did not want to compete with obvious professionals. Two sets of records were initiated and National Championships for both categories were contested each year. Rule changes came frequently to keep pace with growth. As fast as competitors found ways to get around existing rules, new ones had to be formulated to keep things stable. Inequities always exit and change is the essence of racing: rules were constantly in a state of flux and always will be.

In 1925 Johnson Motors came out with its Big Twin. Advertised as a 6 HP motor, it was a 22.5 CID. On 4 July 1925 this motor set a world record of nearly 15 mph. Six months later the record was up to 16.68 mph. Mind-boggling speed at the time!

Through 1926, the typical outboard race boat was a stepless planning boat. Certainly a hydroplane, the boat was usually quite long and narrow with low vertical sides about 6" deep. This type of boat was efficient enough for the low horsepower motors of the day. As motor horsepower increased, the boat s became more sophisticated – the displacement bottom gradually gave way to the one-step hydro. Non-trip chines were seen here and there and then became a design fixture. In the Midwest, the Johnson Motor Company sponsored "Baby Buzzy," which led to this early development, and on the West Coast, the "Elsinore" Hulls built by Buck Holt became famous.

The effort to produce faster, lighter, higher horsepower forced the motor manufacturers to participate in racing during the twenties. As outboard motors proved themselves on the racing circuit, public acceptance followed. The factories spent large sums of money in their racing department proving grounds. The end of the Twenties found the factories selling tuned racing motors, oversized pistons, special propellers, ect.

BOAT RACING - THEN AND NOW

As outboard racing became more complex and sophisticated, the sport developed specialists. Drivers with exceptional talent became prominent. Qualities of judgment, reflexes, co-ordinate, experience and mechanical ability soon produced outboard superstars, as we have today.

This professionalism and the relatively few rules and regulations of the sport produced a decline in racing participation in 1929 and 1930. To meet this problem, the National Outboard Association was founded in 1929. The NOA was supported by the engine manufacturing companies, and an endeavor was made to codify a set of rules which would regulate outboard racing in a sane manner. The NOA racing commission formulated a code which today is standard in all racing associations. Some of the articles:

1- Engine mfg. shall not give, loan or otherwise subsidize racing motors, parts of equipment of any sort to any driver, club or dealer – either directly or by subterfuge, but will require full payment at regular price.
2- Mfg. employees shall not participate in racing.
3- Mfg. shall not pay salary or expense money to any driver, either directly or indirectly.
4- Mfg. shall not advertise racing winnings.
5- Mfg. employees shall not act as a race official unless requested to act as motor inspector.
6- Factor service limited to race day. Service men may not give or loan, directly or indirectly, parts of any sort.

This manufacturer's code ended factory race operations from 1930 to World War II. Factory withdrawal did not adversely affect racing. On the contrary, new life regenerated the sport.

Outboard Marathon played a large part in selling outboard motor reliability and durability. Marathon racing was popular from the inception of the sport. Perhaps because this type of racing did not place a premium on professional excellence, it was very popular with the more amateur participants. Most of the marathons were a free-for-all style. Motors of every size were thrown into the pot and boats of every description were seen. It was colorful both for spectators and participants. Marathons were held on closed courses along rivers, coastal areas and larger lakes.

On the West Coast, the Antioch and Stockton attracted a large following. The tide and lagoon which was to become the Long Beach Stadium and site of the 1932 Olympic rowing events, served as both a closed course and Marathon site. Lake Elsinore, California was a very popular Marathon course. Perhaps the most famous West Coast Marathon was the Sammamish Slough.

The most famous marathon in America, the Albany-New York on the Hudson River originated in 1928. An annual event until 1941, the race was suspended during the war and reactivated in 1947, through 1953. The 125 mile grind sputtered to life again in 1963, then passed into history.

BOAT RACING - THEN AND NOW

Pittsburgh, CA

The Delta region of Northern California has probably long been a haven for all sorts of warm blooded animals including man. The San Francisco Bay is fed by the Sacramento, Napa, Russian and a few other rivers, all coming off the high elevation of the Coast and Sierra Nevada mountain ranges. Throughout the San Joaquin, Napa and Sonoma valley streams, creeks and rivers feed a tremendous volume of water into the Pacific at the Golden Gate.

From the days of paddle, oar, sail and paddle wheel to the modern engines of today, man has used the water system for economic, farming, industrial, and recreational purposes. All the infrastructure needed by the miners of '49 was channeled from the Bay area to Stockton, Marysville, Sacramento and other port towns, then via animal cartage to the miners' camps.

Subsequently, farm products from the cornucopia that was to be the San Joaquin were transported abroad and throughout the nation via the Delta. When transcontinental railroads arrived in 1886 the ports of Stockton, Sacramento, Vallejo, Oakland and San Francisco became great transportation hubs.

Into that land of waterway and beauty entered lightweight inboard engines and the introduction of reliable outboard motors: the foundation of what has become a noteworthy sport—recreational boating.

During the '20's, many outboard motor manufacturers produced engines powerful enough to warrant the design and construction of light weight boats capable of carrying three or more passengers. The boats were most often 13' to 15' feet long, had a double cockpit and were often pushed by a motor of 20 to 40 HP. In addition to the small outboard, a very popular boat was the 15' to 20' cabin cruiser.

Boat clubs sprang up in a good many of the river towns. It was extremely popular for the 15' to 30' boat owners to form a *flotilla* and go from one town to another to celebrate an asparagus festival, an artichoke harvest, ect.

I can remember going from Stockton to Rio Vista for the Asparagus jamboree, where stalks floated down the river one night as we moored along the water front.

1935 Sacramento River

50 Mile Marathon – race what you bring all classes. No handicap two classes one for runabout and one for hydros.

My father, John DeSilva, was a residential contractor in the early 20's. We lived in Pittsburgh, CA which is located along the Sacramento River between Antioch and Martinez. In those days Pittsburgh had a population of approximately 2500-3000. It was originally populated by Italian immigrants who maintained a small fleet of fishing boats operating across the Great Bay into the shallow waters offshore the Golden Gate. At this time in the mid-twenties, they were industrious first and second generation Americans with a strong family ethic.

Housing was in short supply and my father, began building houses. He did well. I have his California K License.

In 1926, he bought what was then the most powerful of the outboard motors, a 4 cylinder, and a small boat. It was not long before John became dissatisfied with the performance of his second hand boat. He would build his own—after all, he was a wood worker. He made some investigation and found a San Francisco boat builder who sold a plan for what some considered a state of the art high speed runabout.

John built the boat, which turned out to be a reasonable performer: probably typical of the time. It was a double cockpit 14' runabout named after his second son, my brother: "Billy boy". The boat was probably better built than the production of the day, which, more often than not, were put together by workers who were more familiar with much larger boats. Still, not easily satisfied, John built a second boat, then a third. Each boat was more a product of his own ideas. Quite soon, others impressed with the workmanship and performance would seek to own one of those new boats.

John's spare time became rapidly occupied in design and construction of these small runabouts for friends and those who were attracted by his workmanship and design.

Then the great depression of 1929 hit John particularly hard because he found himself holding a second mortgage paper which proved to be worthless. He turned to boat building for a livelihood: folks were able to afford several hundred dollars for a small boat whereas they could not financially handle a new house.

I remember one event during the early 20's in Pittsburgh. We were invited to a get together at someone's house. Bill and I were totally unprepared for the sight of what was boiling in a huge pot in the house cellar. After a certain amount of beer, wine and great _____ tidbits, a thing was hoisted out of the steaming pot via a block and tackle. I can still remember the great black rubbery head with a large eye and hanging tentacles. It was a giant squid. It took a brave man to use a sharp knife and hack off a piece from one of the hanging arms. You can bet that Bill and I did not get close to the thing. It didn't even smell good! Nothing looked that evil could be tasty.

Boat Racing: The First Half of the Century

Racing in California during the mid-20's, especially in the Northern California delta area, was a marathon event. Prior to the advent of specific classes, standard boats, and efficient motors, marathons seemed to be the way to go. Start were via a pace boat. Horsepower differential was satisfied by loose handicaps of weight or elapsed time.

Well known professional boat builders of the time in Northern California included Cowden, a Stockton firm (Builder also of commercial power and sail boats); and toward the end of the '20's Zimmerman came into prominence. He had a shop on the estuary of the San Francisco bay off the Bay Shore highway in Oakland. In Southern California the Elsinore was prominent.

By 1930 boat racing on the west coast was in full swing. In Southern California the metropolitan LA area had several hundred competitors; Northern California had about the same.

Outboard racing was divided into two divisions—Professional and Amateur. About this time the National Outboard Association took over as the US sanction of outboard racing. The class structure we have today was created then. The amateur and professional format last until WWII. Inter-Collegiate boat racing of the Ivy leagues was probably one of the main factors keeping the amateur division. Collegiate boat racing never took hold on the west coast, although there were many young drivers involved.

The Cowden runabout was noteworthy in that it had a double-cockpit (Which was

C-105 bounces over the choppy waters of the San Joaquin River, just south of the inland seaport of Stockton, California.

Stockton is one of the two sea served ports of call for ocean cargo ships that carry California's agricultural products all over the world.

The waterway has been used for many purposes – Not least the venue for pleasure boating and racing craft.

Norris Dutcher, c105, was an early pioneer of outboard racing. He developed into a formidable driver- his equipment was first rate and he was aggressive.

C105 was a Zimmerman built boat and one of the first covered front deck runabouts.

typical of the early boats) and high split bow. The Zimmerman lasted until the late 30's. The Rockholt family, headed by Harold, operated a Lumberyard in Marysville, CA. Harold was on hand when several drivers were tested at the downtown lake, and he told his friends that he could built a better boat. He did. From the late 30's through the mid 50's Rockholt was a huge factor in the Alky division.

At Salton Sea in 1947, A George Mishy built runabout appeared which was rather radical in appearance. George was a former eastern driver—a boat builder who moved to Phoenix, Arizona after WWII. He was a 4-60 hydro driver, and a formidable one. The adverse reaction to his unorthodox boat resulted in a set of runabout measurement rules that are in effect today. Harold Rockholt was the senior boat builder at Salton Sea when the set of runabout measurement rules were created. Bud Wiget, chairman of the NOA Alky commission ratified the new rules.

The Alky Nationals in 1931 was held at Lake Merritt, situated in a park within the heart of Oakland, across the bay from San Francisco. Notables on hand that I remember were Jack Maypole from Chicago and RV Collins from Las Angeles. The Collins team members were the two Collins brothers and son Richard. RV drove a hot F runabout and son Richy drove an A hydro. I don't remember who won any of

the championships but I believe the west coast did not fare well.

The original Phantom runabout was built by a man named Shirley, out of Oregon or Washington. The boat was relatively narrow, approximately 30" at the center bottom and shallow non-trip. The boat had only a slight vee and a long keel Overall, it was quite

1938 NOA National Outboard Runabout Championship
Pit Floats at Harrison Lake, British Columbia, Canada
Photo - Photocraft

1931-Long Beach

This is the channel as it was before construction began to ready the site for the 1932 olympic rowing events.

Some of the oil storage tanks and derricks were removed or set back inland in 1932.

C-15 is a Crandal single step hydroplane.

Photo-Lynde

1931 – Long Beach, California

Marathon outboard racing was very popular at this time; using the new big four cylinder motors. Boats were usually 14'-15', double cockpit with a passenger-mechanic outboard. Speed for thee marathon boats was around 35-40 mph.

The camera is looking East, soon to be created Olympic Stadium.

Entrance into the estuary was left

Photo-Lynde

handsome, with a rounded vertical bow and a good amount of tumblehome hull and rounded deck. A formidable racing machine!

Rocky Stone of Willamina, Oregon was probably the most successful devotee of the Phantom especially when the design was taken over by Wilber McDonald in the late '50's. Rocky visited our shop sometime in 1952-53, prior to a scheduled Long Beach Marina Stadium regatta and said, "I'm doing 60

mph with my PR." Now this was in an era when the standard and runabout would go perhaps 54-55 mph.

Bill and I built the first of the box type runabouts in 1954. The era of the banana boat had ended and we wanted to go in another direction. Competition from the Willis comet was such that we had to build a better boat, especially to compete in the east where the course conditions were most often not as favorable as on the west coast.

A mile record speed trial was conducted after the APBA National at Lake Alfred, Florida. 1950 Jack Stanford, the son of a local big time auto

1950 Lake Alford, Florida

The 1950 APBA Alky Nationals was a big event. Teams from over the US were there.

This was not the first post-war Nationals where both the hydro and runabout were scheduled, but it was the first of the true national event where contestants attended from throughout the US. This was proved by winners from desperate areas of the country, Bud Wiget, California (C service runabout), Jack Maypole, Chicago, Illinois (Free-for-all Hydro), Gilbert Peterman,, New York (A hydro), Jack Stanford, Florida (C racing runabout).

The Stanford win created a stir. A number of Florida PR powered boats had lower units with removed cavitation plates – Considered a no, no by most experts. However, Jack Stanford's winning PR had a chopped unit.

The photo shows Harold Abrams, Wilmington, North Carolina working on his PR powered runabout while Bill DeSilva looks on, Ralph DeSilva, kneeling is probably telling Abrams that he needs a boat cart rather than use tin cans.

Photo- Snell.

dealer set a record of 55+ mpg with his Walk Blankenstein built PR65 and Willis comet. The Boat went through the traps with a giant bounce and leap every 100'. But a remarkable speed considering the boat's terrible ride. As a further aside Stanford's lower unit had not Cavitation plate—an innovation locally popular at the time. The no Cavitation plate lower unit was soon found to be a performance flaw, not an advantage.

At the Lake Alfred Nationals, Bud Wiget won the service C runabout championship using a Rockholt runabout and his own home built Evinrude motor. This particular boat was a design Rockholt had used in the years past and not the model sold generally to the public at the time. Bud had been driving one of the new boats at Lake Merced in Madera, California when the boat unexpectedly flipped on the straight while Bud was leading, in relatively smooth water. Now, one can explain the problem by pointing to the very short plane and a very quick dead rise. Bud wanted no repeat of that experience and had Harold build one of the older models which had a more conventional bottom.

In the early 1950's we began toying around with a so-called "Floater" for the stock program. Some drivers in the northwestern had been playing with this type of boat in the all-consuming push for more speed. Now a floater type boat may provide speed—but at a price. In the Alky division we knew that high speeds would not allow the use of this sort of boat. But at the relatively modest speed of the stock division we felt that it might be possible to successfully design something. We quickly found that any speed beyond the power plant of a C stock runabout, a floater would be marginally stable.

Harry Bartolomei at this time was making a name for himself as a premier outboard speed driver. Prior to a Kilo venue at Turlock Reservoir by Modesto Springs, 1965, Harry borrowed our 13' floater in an attempt at the 500 C class Kilo. We set the outfit up and told harry to be careful because he was in uncharted water. Bartolomei was a fearless competitor and entered the trap full bore with his Konig motor in a light water chop and slight cross wind – weather conditions relatively good. He passed the entry buoy about 50' when the boat took off for outer-space. The equipment arrived back at the pits with the motor intact and the boat only slightly damaged. Harry was thoroughly wet but appeared unscathed. About 15 minutes later he suddenly looked at me, shook his head and said, "What happened!" He couldn't remember anything about the episode. The situation ended happily but we sold the floater to a non-racer and left the program as a non-commercial project.

We have had a few non-commercial designs. Some of them were by-products of the ever ongoing attempt for a faster, safer, better preforming boat. Some were merely "ahead of the time."

Ethel and Bud (Clark) Wiget work on their Evinrude C service motor – in the pits at Lakeland, Florida.

This motor was probably the best not built by Tom Newton. Bud often said, "I drove for 7 years before winning a first place, the competition was that good."

It may have taken awhile but Bud became a legend in outboard racing. It was a career of many years and highlighted with all the honors. His record of championships and world records rank with the giants of boat racing.

Meizzie could drive a race boat. She raced everything from an A hydro to a 135 CID inboard.

Ethel and Bug married in 1942 – while each worked in Southern California. They then moved north, where Bud inherited a walnut orchard in what later became downtown Concord.

They purchased the Lakeland, Florida boat shop owned by marshal Eldridge – on Magnolia Ave in 1958. But had decided to retire and spend his days boat racing.

Harry Bartolomie 1961 B Hydro – Lodi, California

Bartolomie began boat racing in 1958. By 1961, he had progressed to the B Alky Class and West Coast rep for the Konig racing Motor.

Boat in background has a Mercury motor driven by Janet Herrick, Sacramento. Although the Bull Nose hydro was moderately successful—Lon Stevens had raised the Service C hydro kilo record to 61+mph – and the design had sold well, use felt the design was a long way from where one wanted to be. Thereafter, we streamlined the front cowl and lengthened the aft plane. There changes helped win the NOA B Alky Championship for 3 straight years.

What about the Speedi-Twin?

The Outboard Motor Company called it the Speedi-Twin. Over the years it has been called many things—sometimes in terms not used in polite society.

One may well ask why the Evinrude C service motor has been so fascinating to so many, for so many years after its introduction in 1931—more than 80 years ago.

The motor should have had no great appeal. It was design and sold as a general purpose motor—not as a great piece of equipment. The Speedi-Twin was sold at an attractive price; with slight improvement over the next 20 years—till production ceased in 1952. It was intended to be a reliable, simple two stoke design with no frills—it was a product of the time. The motor has a number of flaws; fragile connecting rods; a heavy flywheel over a bronze top crankshaft bearing surface; and a bad carburetor.

The Speedi-Twin did have one good thing in its initial favor—a relatively streamlined lower unit. That is probably the one great reason the motor was found attractive by the outboard racing clan.

The motor was popular on the West Coast because of price and horse power. It could push either a heavy craft or a small family pleasure boat.

The Johnson Outboard Motor Company provided a serious competition to the Speedi-twin via their PO model. The Johnson was probably more reliable and easier to start. Its flaw was a terrible lower unit and weak crankshaft. Johnson soon replaced the PO with their P-50 and the battle between the two motors continued long after the Johnson Company merged into OMC in 1934.

A small group of race drivers in Northern California started the C service class. They thought these middle range pleasure motors could push their race boats at a reasonable speed and provide them with another class.

Ward Angilly, Harold Ashley, Duke Ellington, Frank Nunes, Chet Livingston, Andy Laird, Martin Leach, Loyal Oseau, Ugo Perodi and Ernie Millot were all prominent in formation of the C service runabout class. Some favored the P-50 and some used the Speedi-twin.

Ernie Millot was probably one of the first to recognize the possibilities of this new class. The spectator public did not know the difference between a pure race motor and one originally sold as a fishing motor. Soon however, these stock motors began a gradual modification. Muffler chambers were removed in favor of an open exhaust. Over the years, after market suppliers made lower units, gear cases, tower housings and a more efficient Vactori P-500 carburetor was allowed. Over the years, the Speedi-Twin was improved with the use of stronger connecting rods; and a ball/roller bearing could be placed on the upper crank surface instead of the bronze sleeve. Tower housing could be modified so that transom height would be the same for both Racing and C Service.

Although the Great Depression was general in the US, the outboard motors were somewhat of a novelty. They had become reliable, practical and could be the source of great outdoor pleasure.

1948 Northern California Outboard Association San Francisco

Left to Right: Ethel Wiget, Clark (Bud) Wiget, Patricia Wiget, Roy Hansen

Roy Hansen and Patricia were married oon after this happy occasion. Roy drove a very competitive F hydro and runabout for several years. Today they live in Nevada where Roy is retired.

Ernie Millot was an auto mechanic who had moved into outboard motor work at a Stockton boat and motor dealership. He very soon became a prominent motor man and an outstanding boat race driver. His comprehensive written data on these early outboard racing motors was the source from which Bud Wiget later became a national outboard racing icon after World War II.

The Johnson P-50 did provide serious competition for the Evinrude. The two motors each had areas where their numbers were more prominent.

Southern California favored the P-50 while Northern California and the Oregon-Washington areas had a strong Evinrude class.

As these C service motors became popular and motor modifications took place, the class grew at a huge rate. C service runabout became a US national class. First, a national runabout class, C service hydro was only a local event on the West Coast till it became large enough after WWII, that it was also nationally recognized.

The Evinrude Speedi-Twin is today a true racing motor. It is about 5-7 mph slower than the Pr-65 racing motor, but it has its own cachet.

There are Speedi-twin cylinder barrels buried in the backyard all over California and the west Coast- placed there for seasoning. In a century or two, an archeologist will find these artifacts and wonder??!!

The Evinrude fascination is curious. Alex Gomback, Cleveland, OH, spent the winter of 1952, every evening, hand polished the internal fuel passages of his Evinrude. When asked about that, Tom Newton replied, "…probably not much help but it can't hurt."

Tom newton switched from the P-50 to Evinrude in 1939. His job as caretaker of the dam in the foothills above the coast of Santa Barbara gave him time to become a self-taught machinist, welder, foundry man and outboard motor specialist.

During the war years he built a dynamometer and spent hours on the efficiency of his Speedi-twin.

In 1946, Tom purchased a new runabout and in one of the big races that year, he proved that he had found areas of improvement in the Evinrude. Improvement that gave him speed no one thought possible.

In 1948, Manuel Carnakis, Bakersfield, CA, informed us that he was considering a switch to a Rockholt runabout because he was getting beat consistently and thought our boat was responsible.

*****

He started as a stock outboard division driver then moved into the Pro (Alky) ranks when he purchased a 250cc Class A motor from Kay Harrison, Ohio, and a used runabout from Jack Kugler, Illinois.

Peter proved the "old saw" that everyone has a moment of glory when he was able to dominate the class A competition for a considerable amount of time. Boat racing is sometimes marked by a driver who achieves a very high standard – beyond the norm. This domination, historically, does not last long.

A series of Italian motors came along and put an end to Crowley's reign. But for a period of time, he had an outfit that was extremely hard to beat.

Several years before we had introduced him to Maurice Beckman, Cleveland, OH, who had been doing his motor work. Manuel was looking at a speed of about 47 mph on our boat.

We told him that the boat was not his problem. We suggested he take his motor to Tom Newton and have it checked on his dyno.

Sometime late in 1948, we all drive up to Newton's landing in the mountains. One had to drive about 10 miles up a very narrow road to a 2 acre bull-dozed area where a house and outbuildings was located.

The dam was over another hill, about 1.5 miles over a walk path. Tom walked twice a day to the dam where valves had to be checked and adjustments made. Not a lot to do, but important and necessary.

The Carnakis motor was mounted on the dyno and Tom ran the motor till he attained its peak performance. When asked how fast the motor would be expected to be, Tom replied, "About 47 mph." This confirmed our opinion.

Prior to this, Newton had never expected to work on motors for other race drivers. However, when asked how fast Tom could make the Carnakis motor, Tom said, "I can get your motor up to about 52 mph."

Manuel, Bakersfield, CA mayor said, "How much and how soon?" Tom agreed to do the work, Tom probably agreed because they were friends, the money was welcome and he loved working on the Speedi-twin.

After Carnakis received the first re-work, he had Newton do the same with another. For the next 20 years, Manuel won perhaps 80% of races entered and almost never had motor problems. This first transaction started Newton's career as a Speedi-twin motor specialist. To this day, no one has obtained more out of the Speedi-Twin C service motor. An untold number have tried to duplicate Newton's work and have not done so.

Today there are a few drivers who claim they own or drive a Newton built motor. Perhaps this is true, but as Tom said a number of times, "Once the motor leaves my shop and is opened, it will never perform as it did originally." This has proven to be true over the period of more than 60 years.

When asked why they went to the trouble and expense of making a C service lower unit for the Speedi-twin, Both Tom Goslee and Buzz Miller said, "I just want to help."

Tom Newton

Tunnel and East Valley Road started at US highway 1 about halfway between Montecito and Santa Barbara. It was blacktop for about 5 miles up the canyon. For the last couple it was gravel and one way.

Eventually the road ended at a 2 acre roundabout where Tom Newton had his home and shop. He worked for the Santa Barbara Water Company which operated a dam just over the hill. It was an isolated spot but Tom, his wife and two daughters seemed to think the job site was fine.

There was no turnabout area within the last 2 miles of road – it would not have been good to meet an oncoming vehicle – the drop-off down the canyon had to be over 150'.

The County had provided a good size shop. He had all the machinery necessary to maintain the dam's components and his own boat racing hobby. He was a self-taught machinist, welder, foundry-man —he could do anything mechanical and do it very well. And, one could almost eat off the shop floor.

Tom had stared boat racing in 1937, with a Johnson P-50, on a runabout.

He competed with no great success- just a good competitor, with a friendly manner. Prior to WWII,

Tom Newton, 1947

he got hold of an Evinrude Speedi-Twin C service motor. He made a dynamometer and spent countless hours trying to find the motor's capabilities-then forced it to give more than the factory designer's had ever intended. After all, it was a fishing and sportsman motor that had never been intended to become a viable racing machine.

But, there had been thousands manufactured parts available and they were relatively cheap. It was the motor of choice for those who liked to tinker and tune-it enough CID and a gear ratio to carry and good size race boat at a reasonable speed – It was a natural choice to place the Evinrude within the mid-range of the Alky division C service.

Newton bought one of our runabouts when racing began after the war. His immediate performance astounded everyone. He did not just win, he ran away from the field. On every measured venue, he set new records. He went to Celina, Tennessee in 1947 for the National Championships. He won one heat and had a battery or fuel problem in the other. He did not win, but there was no doubt who was a C service star.

Newton stopped driving a race boat in the latter '50's. However, his motors have dominated the C service class to this day. No driver today, using what was once a Newton can attain the speed one once saw in the '50's and '60's.

One can reason that nitro-oxide fuel was at that time legal – not now. At one time, one could see 56mph on the indicator at Depue, Illinois. Today the winning runabout will be hard pressed to indicate 53mph. One has to believe that these old motors are not as good as Newton was able to make them – and that perhaps nitro has made a difference.

Tom Newton is gone. The old iron lives on… It isn't how fast you go, it's the way you play the game!

1955 oil city Louisiana

Left to Right: Dave Barnes, Zanesville, OH (World champion in class C-1 Hydroplane), Bob McGinty, Corpus Christia, Tx (World champion in Class C Racing Runabout), Deanie Montgomery, Corsicana, TX (World Champion in Class A Hydroplane), Homer Kincaid, Carbon Cliff, IL (Winner Class B National High-Point and the "Jack Lockheart Memorial Trophy"(Pictured in front of him). Jim Griffen, Quicy, IL (World champion in Class F Hydroplane, Bill Seebold, Granite City, IL (World Champion in Class C Hydroplane), Ellis Willoughby, Alexander IL (World Champion in Class C-1 runabout). Kneeling Deiter Konig, Berlin, Germany with the Sportsman Trophy and Clay Petterrer and Lake Charles Louisisana with the Tatum Trophy for free for all runabout.

A boat race always results in a few happy winners. Here are a few who came south and are going north with a championship. Bob McGinty will travel only a few miles west of Shrevenport, where he will show his trophy to Harry Marioneaux; his equipment owner.

Homer Kincaid, Caron Cliff, Illinois, mechanical engineer, receives only one of many past and future accomplishments. Few will ever attain his stature in Alky outboard racing. Dieter Konig, Berlin, Germany, has come to America to promote his outboard racing motors. He has also proven to be a good boat driver.

Alexandria, Louisiana 1979 Lake Spivey, NOA Nationals

Four iconic outboard rasing members who will be remembered for excellence. From left to right: Hy Bartelson, IA, Bob Murphy, IL, Bud Cowdery, USA, Stand Leavendusky, KS.

Bartelson was brother-in-law to Home Kincaid and sponsored his racing equipment for many years.

Bob Murphy, plumbing contractor, Springfield, IL, purchased the Newton built C service equipment of the Fred Brinkman team and became a top performer in that class.

Bug Cowdery loved boat racing. He at one time or another campaigned equipment in most all categories of the sport. He was perhaps one of the all-time best racing boat starters.

Stanley Leavendusky, Kansas City, built some of the very best Alky Outboard motors. His equipment especially C Service is currently used and winning today.

The Propeller: A Black Art

When someone once asked Benjamin Franklin about how to predict the weather he answered, "By guess and by God!"

The science of outboard racing propellers can be described in about the same way.

Given the working formula (RPM x Pitch x .095 / Gear Ratio = Speed) one can come up with a ballpark pitch number. But how does one arrive at the propeller possible: number of blades, rake, blade design (Michigan confirmation, cleaner style, Kamic design, Johnson form Stannus shape and so on)?

We no longer have the bonifide genius of the Wright brothers to give us an answer, so we rely upon the expert of the day. Perhaps we should hark back to Allen Smith—the generally accepted master of outboard racing propellers of the post war era. Smith is reported to have said, "Whenever I got to accepting the idea that I was a prop expert I took another look at my working model Stannus and it brought me back to the fact that I know very damn little about props. That prop is a design nightmare — it should not work, but in the 50 years I have been around no other design propeller has seriously challenged its dominance in the C class using the Johnson PR-65. It has no rake, most of the blade is situated in the wrong place and what kind of a shear-pin station is that!?"

Allen Smith is right; the Stannus propellers follow no logic. Yet you can't argue with success. Even today the Stannus propeller can be seen on the winning boat hydro and runabout at the major Alky antique races. The design has been copied by most of the competing propeller manufacturers with little success. One can say that little has changed in basic propeller design within the last 80 years—insofar as the Stannus effect is concerned.

During the early 1930's my father and Ernie Millot would go from Stockton to Oakland (Approx.. 80 miles) where they would gather a few propellers from the Johnson Propeller Co. and test at the estuary alongside the airport. Often Mr. Johnson would accompany them. The unique Johnson style propeller was rather efficient on the racing boats of the day, and especially so on the just-introduced 22HP Evinrude Speeditwin.

Necessarily, over the years, my brother and I had to become knowledgable about propellers: what was currently working best on our boats, and how best to setup.

Most objects of utility, over time, have evolved into one form of efficiency—a certain size or shape. For instance, such a simple object as a spoon is merely a hollow disk of small size, with an attached handle. Vary the design appreciably and the spoon no longer has utility. But vary a propeller in many ways and it still may produce a worthwhile result. A two blade propeller may be as fast down the straight, but perhaps does not accelerate well as a 3-blade. A 3-blade may be fast as a 4-blade, but does not efficiently carry the boat through the turns.

Melvin Cooper is caught in the rooster-tail of a competitor on the approach to the first turn of a B hydro event at the APBA National Alky Championship regatta.
He was able to keep his boat right side up and continue the heat, although not up front. His start in the next heat was better and went home with third place trophy.

More often than not, a boat design will determine the propeller to be used. The modern 3 pt hydro plane will usually require a low rake propeller. The current outboard racing runabouts most often need a propeller with rake. The current stock outboard runabout needs a low rake with a negative prop shaft angle. The present day Alky runabout needs a high rake, multiple blade propeller. Speed differential between these two is a reason for the different propeller requirement.

Speed near the ton does force a measure of stability not necessary on slower boat speeds. The shape, or form, of a propeller has always been a mystery to me. You would think a certain shape would have proven, over time, to be more efficient than another. I have come to the conclusion that one type of propeller or another will work in combination. By combination, I refer to engine, boat, weight, and setup.

Back to Stannus. It works for the old Johnson PR65. It never worked for the Evinrude 22HP C service class. The metrics are quite different. So there's no universal formula here: we work "by guess or by God!"

1946 Needles

In 1946, air conditioned auto were not what they are today. Californians rarely purchased cars with weather relief except for heaters.

We made the mistake of going to an Alky boat race at Needles on July 4th. At that time Needles was a tiny back water village on the Colorado River on Highway 66 (Later to become Interstate 10). There was nothing on either side of the Needles for 60 miles except cactus, jackrabbits and rattlesnakes.

In planning the trip we either forgot or ignored the weather; July in Needles can only be described as extreme. We had recently purchased a vehicle, I think it was a Chevrolet coup (the only car to have at the time!) so we anticipated no car trouble.

1941 — Salton Sea, California

Bill DeSilva watches while Joe Leonardo, Hanford, California changes spark plugs on his Evinrude C service motor. This was one of the last races held in Southern California, prior to WWII.

"My Shadow" Was built in 1939. The boat was typical of that time. Joe's equipment often looked rough but he was a good mechanic and a fine driver. He was always a top contender on the west coast.

We left Barstow about noon and headed into the high desert. About 40 miles out of Needles we encountered a boat on a trailer on the side of the road. We stopped and offered assistance.

Russ Hill, his wife and two sons were waiting for their car to cool off. Jr was about 6 years old and Run was just out of diapers.

The only other thing remembered of that Needles was that Joe Leonardo, Hanford, California won most of the runabout races with his C service motor. Hill's PR was faster but the motor did not like the weather.

At that time Hill was a painting contractor and an enthusiastic boat racer and he was not the expert motor man and tech expert that he later became. In addition, no one know that he had fathered a race boat dunasty through the exploits of his two sons Jr. Hill and young Ron.

May years later at the regatta in Northern California, Russ SR was race motor inspector. He antagonized two drivers through a disqualification who verbally promised to inflict some bodily harm . When told that Ron was on hand, they decided the hard line was not in their best interest. After all, a 6'5", 225lb 25 year old specimen is not someone to ignore in a time of stress.

As this is written, the Hill family is still involved in boat racing.

Design

There have always been two factors in outboard racing, those who favor the hydroplane design and those who would choose the runabout.

It is true that the hydro looks more glamorous—sleek and streamline— the *real* raceboat. In contrast, the runabout resembles the second cousin to a rowboat, a thing in your backyard.

To a purist, the hydro's attractiveness has little merit. If not for less weight per class and runabout restrictions, there would be little difference in performance.

Any design that can plane will do so at three degrees. A barn door will plane off at three degrees. As speed increases that object will require less plane angle to sustain its momentum. When the boat attains the speed which overcomes gravity, the angle will be neutral—the boat then becomes and airplane. Now the fun begins!

1954 Sebastopol California

When hydros first came on the scene in the '20's, they were short, narrow and had no step. The California "Elsinore" hydro in 1930 was a bestseller. It looked typical, except that it had a small non-trip chine (a sharp angle in the hull) amidships. The chine did not go below the waterline.

A short time later, the single step design became popular. During the history of the single step, the front step was always placed below the waterline. This, of course, produced a constant aft plane drag— the rear planning surface could never achieve a

End of an era. 1974 was the year the flat deck runabout ended. It did have a good run – the design was viable from 1954 to 1974.

The Kr (top) took its place. That design succeeded till about 1985 – its bottom design is being used today be alky boat builders.

Speed being attained today through fantastic Alky motors has mandated a strong down pressure deck design – the modern alky runabout has more to do with stability than speed. The speed comes easy, stability does not.

neutral plane angle. That consequence and a short aft plane length cause an excessive up and down movement at speed.

A number of laws govern any high speed boat. The most fundamental is that trim in inversely related to speed: this can't be ignored.

A traditional naval architect will usually throw up his hands when faced with an Outboard, Inboard, or Tunnel race boat. The standards, rules, off-sets and formulae that govern the displacement boat to not apply to a planning race boat.

However, the positive effect of Newton and Bernoulli on planning boat design shouldn't be dismissed.

Dr. V.B. Koriagin walked into the DeSilva shop in 1968. He said, "I'm working on a ground effect project and have a problem in getting the boat rig to achieve sixty miles per hour, which is the minimum I need to get a true ground effect and prove my theory. I'd like to bring the project to you and look the thing over to see what could be done to plane more efficiently." (Ground effect refers to a design meant to counter gravity, with the vehicle in close proximity to its base.)

Dr. Koriagin was an aircraft design specialist who had worked at Lockheed Aircraft for thirty years, and had several design patents. In a 1965 paper titled "A Solution to the High Speed Over-Water Problem," Written by Koriagin and R.T. DeVault, "The status of high speed over-water

1965 Ron Hill

Hill had just won his class at Castaic Reservoir, California, a COBRA OPC regatta.

This boat had been built for the new APBA OPC category. It became the prototype for what later became the MOD VP class,

In essence the

MOD VP is a narrow bottom runabout with a tunnel and sponson on each side. The design proved to be efficient and stable at high speed.

Photo-Delachner

1953 Colorado Marathon,
William Schiefer 446C in a B stock Runabout is leading a flight o boats on the Colorado River at Needles. They will go down river to Topock, 45 miles and return.

Marathon racing became popular when it became clear that stock category motors (Mainly Mercury) were dependable and would withstand marathons adversity.

The Colorado River was perfect for this activity. The water was clean and mostly calm and noise only bothered the jackrabbits – this was desert country.

1952 Snell Racing Team,

Left to right: Albert, John Snell

The twin Snell Brothers began an outboard racing activity shortly after WWII. Their Jasper, Texas area was not an outboard racing bot-bed but the brothers have created a racing museum of motors, parts and boat which is the envy of many racing enthusiasts.

Their work in promotion, sponsorship and officiating racing events in Eastern Texas has created a host of boating enthusiasm

Cleaburn Phelps, Jasper got the racing bug from the Snell's and has sponsored a formidable runabout and hydro powered by an outstanding Mercury 75H motor. His team, crewed by the Snell brothers have campaigned throughout the Southern US very successfully for the last 30 years.

vehicle design is reviewed and it is shown that no efficient design exist in the speed range of 50-150 knots. Moreover, the development of existing designs is not expected to produce significant gains since an order-of-magnitude improvement is needed."

Koriagin noted how, around 1905, Crocco demonstrated the hydrofoil and a few years later, Alexander Graham Bell set a hydrofoil speed record of sixty knots. Technology in the high speed, over-water field has not progressed very far since, wrote Koriagin. Examination of the basic design principles of existing high speed over-water craft showed that no large performance improvements were possible. If truly efficient vehicles were to be developed, a different principle would have to be found.

The only concept known to Koriagin with the necessary potential was the "ground effect flying boat." The process of "planing" on the water's surface, he wrote, is familiar and fundamentally simple. Its application to practical vehicles is not simple, however, and best obtained performance is far short of ideal. In general, the designer cannot hold the trim angle to the ideal, since this would mean shifting the center of gravity with the shift in center of pressure obtain as the speed changes. The low trim angle and large exposed planning area cause severe impact loads at high speed. The dynamic pressure of water at sixty knots in 10,000 lbs/sq. ft.—so that even tiny waves can produce high vertical acceleration a this speed, with attendant serious structural and dynamic problems.

In summary, Koriagin argued, the ground effect flying boat seems to be the only concept that offers the potential of efficient operation in the 50-150 knot speed range over water. On the other hand, no amount of development can make the planning hull, hydrofoil, or ground effect machine truly efficient.

Such was the thinking of one of America's foremost airplane and ground effect experts.

His ground effect machine (GEM) turned out to be a 15' deep-vee fiberglass family type boat with wings, flaps, sponsons, and struts all over. It was powered by a McCulloch 75 hp motor. The package weighed a great deal. We suggested he use a more powerful motor. He replied "I do not want to do that; it would nullify what I'm trying to do, which is to prove the efficiency of a GEM."

The obvious thing was to put a viable planning surface on the boat— widen it to support weight till the ground effect took over. Dr. Koriagin spent several weeks at the shop while the boat was modified. While he was on hand, we had some thoughtful discussions on planning theory and boat performance.

We were informed sometime later that he was able to get his project over sixty mpg, but we never learned whether it proved his GEM theory as applied to a planning boat.

So, we are all doing the best we can with the natural laws and constraints we live with. The more we know of our basic restrictions, the better our effort will be. It is probably safe to say that some reasonable efficiency has been achieved in our racing divisions. Perhaps progress in the future will be modest, but that should not inhibit the effort to make our boats better.

What may be questioned is whether safety issues will keep pace with speed efficiency. While it may be had to find in the usual medical journals, there is a disease caused by the boat racing bug. There is no remedy; it can only be soothed by messing around with a fast boat.

*****

1998

Photo of Motor – Mercury 75H, six cylinder with megaphone pipes. Engine builder Cleaburn Phelps, Jasper behind the motor.

South of the Grapevine: Runabouts and Hydros

In 1936 we were living in Stockton. Father was somewhat of a vagabond—never stayed in one place very long. The great depression was a factor, but he also liked to see what was on the other side of the mountain. We had lived between Stockton and Pacific Grove (Monterey) except for 1925-1928 in Pittsburgh.

John thought Southern California was fertile ground for his boat business. There were no major boat racing builders in the area at that time, except for a couple of inboard racing specialists.

The Elsinore company had stopped building in 1932-33, but boat racing in Southern California was booming. There were probably several hundred active boat racing members south of the Grapevine. Of course there were a few part-time builders. R.V. Collins probably built a few boats each year, and Lawrence Comstock a few less.

Collins was a plumbing contractor. He operated out of a shop on Florence Avenue in Englewood. He, his brother, and son Richard were active in both driving and officiating. Comstock had, at that time, a small boat and motor shop in west Los Angeles. There were also a large number of drivers who raced

1946 Long Beach Marine Stadium

Ed Silva, Hanford, California is on his way to an untimely bath. The boat brand is Jacoby. The camera is looking northwest.

homemade hulls.

Most of the hydros were imported from the East—Jacoby and Flowers. These single step boats were not sophisticated. So long as the boat had integrity, was strong—it would do. More important was the motor, the piece of equipment given the most care and attention.

In the '30's there were motor specialists in most areas of the country who could do expert work. In the pre-war years it was not unusual for most men to be hands-on capable. It was not unusual for a driver to spend all winter, after dinner, down in the basement or garage polishing the intake passages of his motor. I once asked Tom Newton if this was of any great advantage. He replied, "Probably not, but it doesn't hurt!"

Probably the most famous West Coast hydro prior to World War Two was the Elsinore. My father did not think the boat was a great design. He thought the brand was fortunate in having a large number of great drivers. The boat itself was a pointed monoplane, with no non-trip chine. It was really a small runabout.

Another boat of note was the Crandall, of Newport Beach. These boats had a good reputation as racers and their designs were featured in National magazines of the early '30's.

Father's first runabouts were double-cockpit, between thirteen and fourteen feet long, and probably weighed around two hundred pounds. He did not make a non-double cockpit boat until 1929, when he used a batten-linen front deck. He was likely one of the first builders to make a covered front deck runabout. (Herb Rimlinger was one of the first Southern California drivers to buy a runabout built by my father.)

Most boats at this time did not feature non-trip chines. Speed range around forty or fifty miles per hour did not require a sophisticated bottom. Boats used batten-seam construction—and so were big and heavy. Weight in a race boat has always been a factor, but lightweight material and waterproof glue was not available then. Framing was usually Sitka Spruce, with Philippine mahogany or Spruce planking.

Plywood, as we know it today, was not available. Our first pure waterproof plywood was found after World War Two at Howard Hughes' surplus outlet, in Playa Del Rey. This was material from the manufacture of his famous "Spruce Goose."

The very early hydros were only marginally faster than runabouts. They were both mono-planes, but the hydro shorter and much lighter.

My father often talked about the various factors involved in this differential. His preference was always biased toward the runabout, and he only applied himself to a hydro for economic reasons—not for any affection. My preference is essentially the same, but for different reasons.

I agree with my father regarding the pioneer racing boats. The modern outboard racing hydro is a different animal, though. Sponsons on the 3-point enable the boat to plane quickly, which is good. But not all good. A planning object will plane off at the three degree angle, but as speed increases the angle will decrease. Thus there is an inherent drag as speed increases. However, there is another factor involved: the air.

A good 20 CID motor will push a hydro into the area beyond one hundred miles per hour. We should recall that aircraft in World War One flew at eighty-five to one hundred miles per hour and were considered very unstable.

The outboard racing hydro now must be an aircraft on the straight and a boat through the turn. These two factors are not, in a true sense, compatible.

Because the hydro has a forward sponson that helps establish a trim angle, it does not oscillate, as does a runabout. A driver can become comfortable with this seemingly stable ride. And this is when the hydro will bite. As the boat attains speed, the boat will feel stable. But when the air component takes effect, anything can happen.

The modern runabout will always oscillate—that is its nature. As the boat reaches top speed, though, its trim is very slight, with little bow movement. A deck design using down pressure will help the boat maintain a good trim.

During the last few years it has become apparent that the differential between the two basic designs— around the course—is very narrow. Admittedly, the hydro, in contrast to the runabout, looks cool. The term may be pure slang, but it does address the point.

The Great British Columbia Caper

Note: this is a true story. The event occurred about 1931, though I'm not certain of the date or exact details. My father often spoke about the affair when on occasion called for some jocularity, but I was very young at the time and absurdities of the grown-ups then did not hold much interest.

This was in the very early days of the Franklin Roosevelt administration. The Prohibition repeal was about to be enacted but the US had not yet sobered up to its demise.

British Columbia boat racing was not big. But there was enough interest to bring about the organization of a big regatta for the dynamic outboard hydros and runabouts of the day. Enough prize money was promoted to entice a rather large group of Americans.

This was an era in which drinking alcohol was evident in the pits of every race. Alcohol may have been frowned upon by some officials; in fact some advocate absolute elimination of liquid stimulation. However, American reverence for personal freedom seemed to be enough to hold-off such restriction – at least till sometime in the future.

The West Coast has always been noted for its attraction to and use of large motors. A 4-cylender outboard motor had just been manufactured, then approved by the NOA. The ensuring creation of the F class hydro and runabout met with enthusiastic approval by drivers from California up to Washington.

One such motor stuck a piston while being tested by a California driver prior to the regatta. Overnight accommodation and race headquarters were at a downtown five-story hotel of some size and stature. There the subject of the stuck piston came up during evening festivities. The small California group decided that it was possible that the piston could be removed, cleaned and replaced, and the motor be again usable. Yes, but this could not be done in the pits: no light, no power, no facility! Wait, how about the hotel?!

Somehow the motor power head found its way to the hotel third floor. Not easy when five men are involved, in a busy hotel even though late at night. Any inappropriate noise was largely ignored by the boat race group although a number of civilians made known their feelings to management. Loud, Raucous noise may be objectionable but it is manageable—or so it seemed.

Well after midnight the stuck piston had been removed, cleaned and replaced to everyone's satisfaction. But, would the motor run? Only one way to find out. "Let's clamp the motor to the bed-post and start her up! Right, pour a gallon of Dynex in the tank and use the starter rope. Ok, ok. Let Doug pull it over, he's bigger. You pull the spark advance, Ok, Ok. Great, it's going to go. Good, good open the big jet a couple more clicks. Ok, ok. Open the window, there is too much smoke in here and somebody open the door— someone's knocking."

It was said that the police, Royal Mountain Police, fire brigade and ambulance service were all on hand to contain, control and manage what was obviously a major emergency. It was at first thought that a gas explosion had occurred within the hotel or the hotel was on fire or the foundation had crumbled. For a period of time it was difficult to get the hotel guests back into the structure for there was a residue of smoke and strange smell.

Next morning, which was not long in coming, the five Californians were standing before the magistrate who said, "This is the most outrageous situation I have ever encountered. I have never seen a more irresponsible action by a few who are thought to be or considered to be good citizens."

He charged the group with disturbing the peace and half a dozen other offenses. Bail was set and the group left the court and British Columbia.

I'm not sure if the warrant for their arrest is still in effect, but I do know that each individual in this affair never returned to Canada. One, an airline pilot, was careful not to take a plane north of the US. I do not know if all the participants are still alive but there is no reason to name the five—their claim to fame had to lie in other directions.

Note: Collectors should remember that the British Columbia affair occurred some 79-80 years ago and the chances of finding a very early 4 cylinder Evinrude racing motor in a crime storage area of a crime depository would probably be remote.

The Playboy

"Being a playboy is hard work." This was often repeated by Bill Guasti. He was the second son of one of the ancestors who had founded the huge Guasti Wine Company located somewhat south of Hondo Lane's San Dimas ranch (Think of Louis L'Amour's novel *Hondo*), in San Bernardino county.

Bill grew up and went to school among the wealth and high society of the Hollywood, Bel Air, and Beverly Hills crowd. He knew everyone. He had a family friend who operated one of the most successful model and talent agencies, and so knew all the girls including the new ones who came to town. Bill was a natural. He could have played the playboy part in any movie. He was, as Mae West described it, "tall, dark, and handsome."

But Bill did not spend all his time chasing women. His financial interests were wide and varied. He owned and operated a large Boat & Motor Sports enterprise in the San Fernando Valley. After a damaging fire had swept over the Hollywood hills, he drove over the area to observe the devastation spotted a woman who was standing in the street looking at the burned-out site of her home. He stopped for a chat and ended up buying the property. The original house plan had been placed in storage, which enabled Bill to duplicate the house on its original foundation.

He had started driving a 135 CID racing inboard in the late '50's. He once drove to Parker, Arizona for a boat race. Parker sat by at the Colorado River on the southern border of the huge Hopi Indian Reservation. At the time, Parker had a population of about 3,000 with very few public accommodations. Bill knew an opportunity when he saw one. He purchased a number of town lots and over a few years built several apartment rental units.

Bill became the West Coast distributor for the Cary brand of racing propellers. The Cary propeller line was created by Joe Mascari of Long Island, New York, who was the US importer of propellers manufactured by the Radice Company of Milano, Italy. The propellers were expertly made of superior stainless steel (though they did rust!)

Bill asked us to help him sell the outboard propellers he received from Mascari. We had no trouble doing so because the props were superior in every way. We sold lots of them.

At one point my brother Bill had worked up a good Johnson bronze C service propeller which was sent to Italy to be copied in Steel. Sometime later we received twelve beautiful propellers. Manuel Carnakis bought one, and tested at Hart memorial Park in Bakersfield. He phoned immediately, exclaiming, "I've picked up about 1-1/2 mpgh with that new prop—save me another!" The two props subsequently won five or six National Championships for Carnakis over a period of more than twenty years. In 1956 he loaned a Newton Built motor and Cary propeller to Henry Wagner who won the APBA C Service Hydro National Championship at Long Beach Marine Stadium. We ordered another twelve propellers from Italy, which were good but slightly less efficient than the first.

Bill had us design a 12' utility runabout/per the photo. He reported the little duck-boat sold well, and wanted us to design a progressive 15-16' pleasure runabout—however we were completely swamped with racing work and could not devote the time to that effort.

*****

1998

Lake Buhlow photo may now be only a memory of boat racing history.

Earl Mitchell, Texas comes out of aturn at lake Buhlow. He was a long time driver of Cleaburn Phelps' equipment.

Action coming out of a turn at Lake Buhlow. Driver is Dewayne, Texas with equipment owned by Cleaburn Phelps, Jasper, Texas. Motor is a Mercury 75H on a DeSilva KR runabout.

Left- Stanley Leavendusky, Kansas City, Kansas
Middle- Paul Hanes, Thayer, Missouri
Right- C. Jones (Doc), Pheonix, Arizona

1956 Long Beach Marine Stadium

He was Polish. Had to be, his name was Leavendusky – Pure Polish.

But Stanly was about as American as one could get. He wore farmers overalls and spoke English with that flat med-west argot that told you he was far removed from the old country.

He tended a 10 acre peach orchard and tenant farmed a corn patch or two. But his main interest and passion was working in his home machine shop – making parts and fine tuning outboard motors such as the Johnson Pr-65 and the Evinrude Speedi-twin. He made and sold pistons for all these motors, including the German Konig, Later on when it became popular.

We were fortunate in selling Stan a runabout early on for he could drive a race boat better than most and many drivers followed his equipment choice.

We drove through Kansas one year and he introduced us to Dick Neal, who had a shop on Troost Ave in Kansas City. As a result, we became California dealer for his boats and he helped us sell runabouts in the mid-west.

Stanley had a lot of stories to tell – all about some colorful character. One had to do with an old farmer who had a fondness for river catfish. Now, if one likes catfish and wants a steady diet of same, there is a problem – the fish do not often cooperate in being caught.

However, the old man arrived at a solution – a foolproof solution. He had heard about a contraption that assured a steady, sure supply of catfish.

The components were not earsy to obtain. A crank telephone had become obsolete – Had been since the '20's yet, there were a few around - one just had to look hard. A battery was no problem. All one had to do was go out into the river, hook up the battery to the telephone, throw out a line or two and crank away.

Quite soon a number of stunned fish would appear and all one had to do was haul them aboard. This was great except for one thing – the game warden's did not think the sport was legal. In fact the fine was heavy!

Stan assured us that he had never engaged in such activity but seemed to know of those practiced such activity on a regular basis – mostly after dark when any sensible law officer would expected to get some well-earned rest.

In fact, "would you fellows like to have a catfish steak for dinner tonight? I've got some in the deep freeze."

Although Stanley and his son Jr. were very successful competitors, they had one obsession. Their main competitors were the Seebold's.

Stan said, "I can't tell you how many times we were in front, had the race about won when something would break or get loose and the Seebold's would go on to win!"

Despite Stan's lament, his reputation stands today as a standard for other's to emulate. Here is a man among men, rarely matched and never to be forgotten by the outboard racing fraternity.

Photo: 1956 APBA Alky National, Long Beach Marine Stadium

From left to right: M.G. Chestor (Pitcrew), Melvin Cooper, Jack Stanford, Dub Parker

The deep South has produced a good many fine boat race drivers but none better than the above three.

With hand on motor, Melvin Cooper, with helmet is Jack Stanford and next to him is Dub Parker.

Cooper Albany, Georgia, started driving Alky outboards while in high school after some short time in the military, he and his father campaigned runabout and hydro all over the US. He won consistently against all the hot-shots. Today, he and his Melvin Jr. boat race when they can find time away from their job shop metal business.

Jack Stanford, Orlando, Florida, son of a big Florida auto dealer, also began boat racing prior to WWII—but got seriously involved after the war ended. He set a new kilo record with a Willis comet runabout at the 1950 APBA Nationals. His PR-65 ran 56+mph. One can look back and grin at the speed, but at the time, it was thought to be terrific.

When Dub Parker, Gadsden, Alabama showed up at a boat race, one knew that he would probably be the one to beat. Dub was a great starter and always had outstanding equipment. He could drive either a runabout to hydro with equal elan and gusto. Who can forget his Dubinsky hydro!   -1962 St. Petersberg, Florida

Whereas the southern US has never had the large number of northern competitors, the ability of it's drivers has never been in question. The Southerner's have probably had to have more hands on capability because most of the manufacturing and technical expertise has been north of the Mason/Dixon line.

The Puddle

The official name was Lake Los Angeles. Situated on the south side of Washington Blvd., between Venice and Playa del Rey, it was a very small lake created by run-off from Ballona Creek and a small amount of ocean tide water. Lake Los Angeles was about 250 yards long and slightly less in width. On the east side was a county dump; on the west a narrow strip of land shouldered the ocean. The only beach was a boat ramp built by the county.

In 1952 a local Los Angeles TV station promoted a six week outboard racing program at the Puddle. This was a perfect situation for the newly created APBA Stock Racing program—the motors were reliable, plenty of boats participated in each class, and great publicity was promised for all. What a deal!

There first series went well. Public acceptance of the sport was good, and the audience gave the program a very high Sunday rating. The lake was small enough so that the TV cameras were able to give the viewers a very close shot of all the action. It was quickly found that the course required from six to ten boats in each heat, which was okay because the Stock boats were mostly equal in speed, and thus there was plenty of action and water spray.

Another series followed after a short interval. Public reaction was excellent and the ranks of Stock outboard racing in Southern California multiplied. Most public viewers had never seen a boat race and here was an activity that looked very exciting, and not terribly expensive.

But a problem arose. During the second series, a good many drivers found that boat racing every Sunday for many weeks soon took more time, effort, and expense than they anticipated. Although the TV station would have continued a boat racing program, they recognized the basic problems. No further TV was ever again attempted in the LA area.

The Puddle was, except for Long Beach Marine Stadium, the only nearby boat test site for any LA area inboard or outboard race boat. These two sites were always very busy—plenty of activity.

One Sunday we were at the puddle to watch some race boat testing. Ray Harris at that time was a novice—he had a pumper 4:60 and a well-used Collins runabout. My brother Bill went around the course several times as the deck rider. I was invited to do the same. Curious about the Collins, I put on a life jacket.

The boat ride down the straight was a rather violent side to side movement together with a rapid, high, circular, up and down bow action. Rather curious! However, the boat had a rather wide bottom, shallow and small non-trip chines, and, of course, the big, big propeller.

We went down on straight, another, then entered a turn. The boat did not lock up, but continued its dance. Somewhere in the middle of the turn I found myself drinking water. Not having experienced one before, I was amazed how quickly the flip occoured. Except for the untimely bath, no damage was done.

BOAT RACING - THEN AND NOW

Harris soon decided that the Collins boat was not a good F runabout and got one from us. He and his brother Richard then went up to Washington State and won a Pacific Coast Championship.

The Puddle is no more. The dump is long gone. The whole area was dredged to accommodate large power and sail boats, and then was developed into what is now the great Marina del Rey. Shops, Marinas, fine restaurants, high rise condos, and huge office buildings have replaced the old swamp area.

Mt. Carmel, Illinois - 1958 NOA Nationals

C Runabout - PR Motors
Y-60 - Ellis Willoughby - Champion
Y-66 - Paul Hayes
S-12 - Alex Gomback
R-21 - Rocky Stone — PHANTOM BOAT

Iron Port

It was a soft drink. There was no iron in it and it was not alcoholic. There are probably few in the world now who know of Iron Port.

I was seven or eight at the time; we lived in Stockton, which is second only to Sacramento as a great inland port of the San Joaquin Valley.

Several times a year my father would go the 80 miles from Stockton to San Francisco to view the latest Vaudeville at the Palace Theatre. There were no bridges between Oakland and the city at the time. However, there were several ferry operations with which to make the crossing. The main line was located at the foot of 7th St. in Oakland.

On the North-west corner of 7th and Central there was a tavern-saloon. We usually arrived there about lunch time. This was one of those public institutions that have been around for so long that no one remembers when it began. The bar was long, of polished Mahogany, which a brass rail and shined spittoons. At the far end were the barbecue pits. Here were the huge roasts turning slowly.

The sandwich was made with huge slabs of beef, ham or chicken/turkey between great slices of gravy-drenched bread. No Mayonnaise, lettuce or tomato. Just bread and meat—plus a pickle, sweet or dill!

To top this adventure in eating with their Iron Port was perfect. The soft drink was unlike anything- a bit tart, velvety smooth, with a tang but no bite. Cola is a drink—Iron Port was an experience! And, with the boat ferry crossing the bay, sometimes in fog, the 45-50 minute trip was an adventure not to be missed by any young kid.

Sometime in 1973, I was in Oakland with Harry Bartolomei, and I told him about the pub at 7th and Central Ave. Born and raised in the Oakland area, he had no knowledge of the tavern. So we went over to the site. There is was—still operating and doing terrific business.

They had enlarged their food operation, with tables and waiters. Meat was still being cocked over the revolving hot spots. We ordered sandwiches and I asked for an Iron Port. The waiter laughed. He said, "You must be an old customer. We haven't had Iron Port for about 15 years, and I have been working here for 20. We don't get a lot of young customers who want a soft drink and the stuff was hard to make. We made it here, in the back, you know. I don't know the formula, but I suppose it is around somewhere."

I hope it is. I'd like to think that sometime Iron Port would be available to give the pleasure that we once had.

*****

1999 DePue Illinois

Three Alky runabouts of the modern era. Class A (250 CC) boats as they approach the first turn at the APBA Nationals. The Yellow leading the boat is a DeSilva, the others are Kriers.

These boats have a prominent forward deck design with which to control anti-pitch a high speed. Modern Alky motors wind up to a very high RPM, which requires a small diameter and low pitch propeller, this also contributes to stability.
There are not minimum weight requirements in the Pro (Alky) division. There have been consequences for this weight rule, placed a burden on heavier body weight drivers who many not accept speeds of the larger classes but cannot go down in class of lower horsepower because of their heavy weight.

It is generally accepted that an addition of 30 lbs will decrease speed one mph.

Jack Kugler, driver of V100 won two heats of the above race but jumped the gun in another to place an overall third.

The Collins's

The Collins family were big in Southern California outboard racing in the early days, the 20's and 30's.

R.V. Collins, the patriarch, was a forceful, dominant, talented personality. Other members were not shortchanged. Most of the brothers started earning a living as plumbers, and because the area was booming they did quite well.

They did even better as bootleggers. R.V. said, "If probation had lasted a few years longer, I would have been a millionaire. I had only one problem: I couldn't control the smell! The still for making the product was no problem. I could make pure 180 degrees blind folded, and my recipes for gin, whiskey, Bourbon and Rye were great. I never did get rum down exactly, but I was working on it. I moved often enough to keep out of jail—most of the time. Sure, I spent a little time, in the 'cooler', but the penalties were not that bad, especially after I learned to cooperate with the authorities."

I don't know how or why the Collins became involved in boat racing, but at the NOA 1930 National Outboard Championships at Lake Merritt in Oakland, California, they were very much on hand. R.V. drove the F hydro and runabout. One of the other brothers drove C hydro and runabout. Fourteen year old son Richy drove A hydro.

It was widely reported at the time that one of their customers had trouble driving one of R.V.'s hydros and complained to R.V. He said, "Let me get in the boat." After testing it, he came back and said, "The boat is perfect. What the hell is the matter with you? You can't drive a boat for *%?#!" Customer relations was not R.V.'s strong suit.

Richard drove successfully for a few years while attending school in the area. He graduated from UCLA and then interned at a prestigious east coast medical school. Doc spent some time in Korea during that war. He was always reticent about his MASH medical adventures, but one can be sure that it was not without some fun and games.

After establishing a successful practice he again became involved in boat racing when his two sons became of age. They started in the stock outboard APBA. R.V., of course, built their boats. And good ones they were. The kids were very competitive in various classes while growing to maturity.

A fellow came into the ship one day in the early 60's. He was from Colombia, South America, born of an American father and native mother. While living in Colombia, he had become an importer of the German Konig motor. He had immigrated to the US and wanted to sell two motors he had been unable to sell in Colombia.

We contacted Doc Collins who immediately bought an A Alky motor of the latest design, at a reasonable price. This was the first motor in the Alky racing program that Doc Collins employed to commence one of the most successful careers in boat racing.

His first driver was Ted May, then Alan Ishii took over. We did not get Doc into a runabout until his father was unable to provide a hull due to physical problems. May was perhaps a bit too volatile for Collins' strong personality. However, young Ishii proved a perfect fit for the team.

1948 Ted May

He first appeared at the Puddle. Lake, Los Angeles was a small tidal lake alongside a county dump site off Washington BLVD in Venice, California.

Ted had a fun boat. It was a very small saucer shape hull powered by a small outboard motor- he was having fun doing crazy spins amid the more structured class racing boats.

It did not take long for May to become a dedicated boat race driver. The stock racing program held his interest for several years; he then moved into Alky and OPC programs. Sometimes he campaigned with his own equipment – as his ability and experience progressed he began driving for sponsors.

Doc Collins and Ted combined during the 60's – The combination produced outstanding results...at the Alky Midland, Michigan Nationals in 1962, they won the 250cc runabout championship. It was hard to keep them out of a trophy at any big event.

Alan Ishii was no stranger to boat racing. His father had driven a runabout for several years prior to WWII. They operated a machine job ship in S. Main Ave in LA. During the 60's and 70's the Collins team successfully participated in APBA and NOA regattas throughout the US.

Alan married and started a family; Doc was forced to find another driver who turned out to be

Ted was an OMC factory driver in their effort to compete with Mercury in the outboard pleasure Category (OPC). He was lead driver when OMC took the team to France for the Paris Six Hour Marathon in 1965 and 1966.

There have been many "characters" in boat racing – none more iconic than Ted May

Bill Rucker, a Northern Californian who grew up within a racing family. His father, William, Dr. was one of California's prominent drivers. He had started with stock outboards and then became involved in the Alky division. Bill Sr. was a fine driver of both hydro and runabout. He specialized in the larger Alky classes, usually with Mercury motors. When the Konig was dominant he went in that direction. Bill Jr.

was just a younger version of his father. His association with Collins was not to last for they lived some distance apart and business constraints became a burden.

In order to more fully occupy his time after retirement as a medical doctor, Collins became a propeller entrepreneur. He had spent a ton of money with Allan Smith of Shrevenport, Louisiana, and through his expertise began to sell a good many props. Not one to spend days working over a grinding-sanding machine or pounding on a pitch block he found others to do so. He was a great salesman. At one time he was probably selling more propellers than anyone else in the alky and stock divisions.

This is Wayne Baldwin at speed. He is speeding through a Kilo run at the legendary Traps set up at Yelm, Washington.

Wayne drove the higher powered hydro. He wanted to go fast. He was always in the front rank – the results were excellent. His father was always there for help and sustenance.

Alice, Texas, was their home. They raced all over the US and Europe for a generation – the results are legendary.

2005

A Convert to the APBA Antique Pro (Alky) Division from stock ranks, Tim Weber has found the Alky both a challenge and Frustrating.

In as much as the old Antique Motors are no longer being made and the "old time" experts have passed on, one has to learn how to become competent via a "hands on" method.

Weber has both Johnson PR-65 and C Service Evinrude motors. He has made some progress as a mechanic and his driving skills go back to experience gained through tutoring from his grandfather, Williams F. Leutner, Racine, Wisconsin – 1911 – 1990, who was an outstanding race boat driver.

Tim also has stock and modified equipment – which he uses to keep sharp while awaiting Alky antique events.

4:60 Wide Cockpit

When the antique outboard racing program was organized in 1983, there was some interest to again use the 4:60 as one of the classes,

During this period, Westerman Jones, a lifelong devotee of the motor, ordered a runabout for the class. F runabouts build in the '30's, '40's and for a short time in the '50's were all of the traditional ride rear cockpit designs.

The above photo is of the completed boat. The class never became viable and interest soon faded away.

The two-main runabout is still a requirement in the pro (Alky) division 1100 class. However the driving mode is the tandem affair, with the driver forward.

Chet Livingston, Stockton, California became famous in the '30's for his ability to stand on his head while crossing the finish line after he and Ernie Millot had won an F runabout heat. This was an amazing feat, for it is extremely difficult to merely hold on to the deck of the bouncing runabout, let alone do so while doing a head stand.

1987 New Jersey
Can a Deep-Vee runabout make it in the modified division? Answer – Yes and no!

Anything that is not generally accepted is not to be considered a viable product. While in California a few Deep-Vee boats were built for customers in the OPC division of the APBA.

A prototype Deep-Vee was built for use in the APBA modified division. It was acknowledged that a general driver acceptance was not possible, but that a few might favor such a design.

This type boat does require a driver technique for success. The boat will perform satisfactorily only when the driver is able to keep the boat planning on the very narrow bottom pad – and that is not easy to do.

Are there any performance advantages for the design? History indicates that there may be none. The boat has only been successful when high horsepower motors are used and rough water capability is quite good.

Bill Fales, New Jersey liked the design and bought the experimental boat. He put a 44 CID Mercury on the transom. He and son Rick drove the rig successfully for years, in the New England Mod circuit.

Rick established an APBA modified competition record with the outfit at a Dayton, Ohio regatta in 1988.

1964 Richard O'dea Lake Buhlow, Alexandria, Louisiana

O'dea, Patterson, New Jersey began boat racing with an A stock runabout when the APBA stock program started in 1947. He later concentrated his boat driving to the hydro.

Dick became a legend. He was fascinated with boats and motors and became a guru for those who wanted someone to help them progress in the sport of boat racing. His shop became the HQ for North-East boat racing.

He tried boat racing in Europe and came back as the importer of the Swedish Crescent outboard racing motor. He got it approved as the APBA stock division super C class.

Most of his driving talent was devoted to the hydro and especially the larger Alky and stock-modified classes. His later years were largely devoted to motor work and doing research and development for shops worldwide.

This group represents – Depicts a good many of Alky Outboard top talent in the immediate post WWII era. Neither US coast is on hand – this is a select group from the country's heartland. Tenney, Maypole, Kincaid and Vincent are legendary – the rest of the group are top talent.

Milford Harrison is the only driver to throttle with his right hand and turn with his left. Harry Voghts drive only the big hydros – with outstanding success. Clem Landis drove very well, but is most noted for his ability to sleeve a motor cylinder.

Photo- Herberg

1947 Lake Mead Nevada

Hovey Cook, Anaheim, at the starting line of an F Alky runabout heat, Lake Mead, Nevada. Ollie Hyde is his deck rider. The motor is a 4/60 CID Pumper (Evinrude). The boat was built in 1940 by John DeSilva and sold to Cook after WWII in 1945.

Photo credit - Hitchcock

Motor Men

At one time the U.S. had numerous outstanding motor specialists. Prior to World War Two boat racing was a relatively major sport—publicized by radio, newspapers and magazines. While not major sports, Gold Cup Inboard and Outboard racing National Championship events were given some national play. So there was enough activity in racing to enable a number of motor experts to be economically successful.

Tom Newton's major source of income was that of a reservoir manager of a dam which provided water for the Santa Barbara environs. After World War Two his personal motors were so obviously superior that he soon had a great reputation as a motor artist.

About this time Walk Blankenstein came out of the Chicago area as a fine motor mechanic-machinist. His specialty was all phases of the Alky outboard motor. I have also previously mentioned Henry Fuller, the rotary valve specialist. Henry provided general machine work and some after market motor parts.

Stan Leavendusky operated a peach orchard in Kansas City and he also found time to drive a top flight C Service and PR runabout. He was pressured to offer machine and motor work to fellow boat racers because of his own superior equipment. His motors, together with the Newton parts, were the glue that held the C Service class together from the '50's through the '70's.

Stan, together with Rocky Stone, probably were the first two drivers to attain the elusive sixty mile per hour mark with their PR-65 powered runabouts. Stone operated a small stud mill in Willamina, Oregon, and drove a Phantom runabout. He had been one of our first out-of-state customers.

The Phantom brand of racing runabout came along after World War Two. Charles Shirley, of Oregon, is believed to be the designer-builder of the brand. He may have built boats other than the C-Service and racing runabout, but they were not of great notice. For whatever reason Mr. Shirley stopped construction of his boat the then Wilbur MacDonald took over. MacDonald was a great friend of Stone. The two made a great team for many years. Rocky proved that the boat was a reliable performer and Wilbur already showed his great workmanship.

The Phantom was a handsome boat. It had a nicely rounded bow and the sides blended into the deck in a pleasing manner. It also had a long straight keel which required a kick-out to make the boat ride free. The boat turned well, but the shallow non-trip chine presented problems in rough waters. Still, Rocky Stone knew the boat thoroughly and was able to get the best from the design.

1947 Tom Newton
Tunnel and East Valley Road started at US highway 1 about halfway between Montecito and Snata Barbara. It was blacktop for about 5 miles up the canyon. For the last couple it was gravel and one way.

Eventually the road ended at a 2 acre roundabout where Tom Newton had his home and shop. He worked for the Santa Barbara Water Company which operated a dam just over the hill. It was an isolated spot but Tom, his wife and two daughters seemed to think the job site was fine.

There was no turnabout area within the last 2 miles of road – it would not have been good to meet an oncoming vehicle – the drop-off down the canyon had to be over 150'.

The County had provided a good size shop. He had all the machinery necessary to maintain the dam's components and his own boat racing hobby.

He was a self-taught machinist, welder, foundry-man —he could do anything mechanical and do it very well. And, one could almost eat off the shop floor.

Tom had stared boat racing in 1937, with a Johnson P-50, on a runabout.

He competed with no great success- just a good competitor, with a friendly manner. Prior to WWII, he got hold of an Evinrude Speedi-Twin C service motor. He made a dynamometer and spent countless hours trying to find the motor's capabilities-then forced it to give more than the factory designer's had ever intended. After all, it was a fishing and sportsman motor that had never been intended to become a viable racing machine.

But, there had been thousands manufactured parts were available and they were reltively cheap. It was the motor of choice for those who liked to tinker and tune-it enough CID and a gear ratio to carry and good size race boat at a reasonable speed – It was a natural choice to place the Evinrude within the mid-range of the Alky division C service.

Newton bought one of our runabouts when racing began after the war. His immediate performance astounded everyone. He did not just win, he ran away from the field. On every measured venue, he set new records. He went to Celina, Tennessee in 1947 for the National Championships. He won one heat and had a battery or fuel problem in the other. He did not win, but there was no doubt who was a C service star.

A year or two later we got a call from Manuel Carmakis, Bakersfield, who said he was considering the purchase of a Rockholt runabout because he was getting beat and thought that our boat was the problem. He had, for years, been using the motor work of a Cleveland mechanic.

The Old Man and the C

We first met Dave Bryan sometime in the early '60's, when he started Stock Outboard racing. At that time he was a dry-wall contractor in Eastern Los Angeles County around San Bernardino and Hemet. The area was booming then and he was doing well in the housing market.

Dave was probably at one time an Okie. Born in Oklahoma sometime in the late '30's his family later moved to California—at that time, the Promised Land. A steady influx into the Golden state had begun during the gold rush in 1849 and had not diminished.

As a youngster and after high school, Dave chanced into the construction industry. He wandered here and there, apprenticing as a carpenter, cabinetmaker and drywaller.

Southern California became his habitat, especially around San Bernardino-Hemet, part of the great post-WWII population explosion. Somehow he ran into a covey of stock drivers,—notably Wade Terrill and Bob Davidson—in that sub-desert California area and quickly became enamored with boat racing.

For many years Dave raced in the lower horsepower stock program, driving boats built by Terrill and himself. He preferred runabouts, especially C Stock, and quickly established a reputation for superior driving ability. Russ Hill, whose two sons Jr. and Ron had participated in the stock program since its inception, became a top motor mechanic and did most of his engine work. Warren Litton probably helped in an early effort to obtain a good propeller. Dave had learned early on that hands-on policy was the best way to progress. He ordered Michigan propellers in quantity, worked on them, tested them, and eventually developed a system that worked.

He may have driven a hydro a time or two, but was essentially a runabout driver. There is a truism in outboard boat racing: those who start racing in a runabout will subsequently be able to drive anything, whereas those who start with a hydro will subsequently be able to drive a hydro!

Dave was a good craftsman. His home-built boats were examples of fine workmanship, a talent that had grown with some trial and error. He once built a house on speculation: "I once build a spec house with a large upstairs area and decided to live in it till it sold. I quickly learned that was a big mistake for several reasons, not the least was that there was a large frustration involved. Whenever I wanted something it was always on the wrong level. The exercise may have been for my health, but that was off-set by a choleric disposition."

In 1966 the Stock Marathon championship was held on the Colorado River, at Needles. We had built a BU runabout for Paul Kalb, in Michigan, to be first used at the event. He arrived with Fred Miller, who also had a B runabout. Fred claimed he was doing well and expected to win. They were both veteran marathon drivers, among a large contingent of drivers from east of the Rockies.

Kalb showed us his propellers. My brother Bill looked at them and said they would not work on our boat. Paul did not have any Michigan steel props which we know would work on our boat. Bill asked Dave Bryan if he had any spare B Michigan propellers that he would sell. "Sure," Dave replied, "The price is fifty dollars." The deal was made and Paul went off testing. A short time later he came back and said he had picked up two mph, but the propeller had broken a blade. Another deal was made: fifty dollars. More testing with the result of another one mph, but another broken prop. Another deal, another fifty. "I picked up another one-half mph," reported Paul in exasperation, "and this time the propeller better not break because I'm running out of money!"

In the Marathon Roy Miner won the BU runabout, but Paul Kalb finished third. He later said, "I've often wondered how fast I could have gone had my money not run out, and had Dave Bryan propellers to sell!" But the result was not bad for a new outfit running against some of the best equipment in the US. Paul was happy and Dave was $200 richer!

Dave campaigned with some success over the years. His main ambition was to win a National Championship. He had done about everything one could do in boat racing yet he could not put together that combination that would crown all his effort.

He came up to our shop in Sabastopol, California sometime in 1978 and we discussed his problem. Sometime prior to that we had built a series of larger stock runabouts that had been somewhat successful. At this time you couldn't sell a stock runabout unless it was a chine-turner. We live in a monkey-see, monkey-do world and that was the music drivers wanted.

Bryans problem was not that he could not build a good boat. His workmanship was outstanding. Some years prior to all this he had constructed a row of benches in his workshop garage. They were probably as fine an example of workmanship as one could find anywhere. And over the years he had worked on propellers to such good effect that he was considered a guru.

A race boat, a good one, is the product of a combination. A combination of qualities which will provide speed, stability and good turning. Dave's boats were pretty good in general but did not have the complete combination which would have allowed his driving capability to prove itself.

What to do? We told Dave that we could build him a boat with which to win a National. However, he would have to overcome some traditional boat racing ideas. The first this was to forget about that last 1mph that everyone had or was looking for. The second was not to have a boat that required the prop shaft to be placed at a negative angle to make the boat stable enough to get down the straight without going to the moon. We warned him that our runabout would not be the Kamikaze type of his competition. As professional builders we had always refused to sell a boat which we felt was inherently hazardous.

Our boat would perhaps not show the ultimate in speed, but would compensate with acceleration, rough water capability, and good handling around the turns. He would have a chance to get to the turn first, after a fine start. No one would pass in the turn; then it would be up to him to fight it out as the race progressed.

We built him a boat prior to our move to Georgia in 1980, and a second boat in 1981. The Stock Nationals in 1983 was at Oroville, California, where the venue is a huge reservoir on which a 1-2/3 mile race course can be placed. The water conditions can be rough because the site is open in the vast foothills of the Sierra Nevada mountains—wind is most often a factor.

Dave's competition was probably faster in boat speed. However, Dave had very good punch and rough water ability. He managed good starts each heat, got to the first turns as we all planned, and won without great pressure—the C Stock APBA National Runabout Championship.

Today Dave is living the good life. He is retired and spending most of the time near the beach in Southern California. He has not given up interest in boat racing, and with his buddy Ron Hill often attends the odd race. He also makes some great two blade propellers for friends in the Antique classes of Alky Outboard racing. There are probably very few in the US who can tweak a two-blade prop better than Dave Bryan.

Frozen Eyeball!

In the early '60's we received a phone call from H.L. (Fuzz) Nichols. He said "I'm in L.A. now—have taken a position with Coin Meter Washer Service, in Long Beach, and want to get involved with your local racing club; to be of some help."

We had sold a boat to him the previous year. He had two sons who were then at the University of Minnesota, St. Paul. Dave, the elder son, was the lead driver; Phil, his backup.

We asked whether the two sons would join their parents. Fuzz replied, "Yes, as soon as the present semester is over they are coming." Some months later the boys arrived and resumed their racing activity.

Upon receipt of our first unfinished runabout, they had converted a basement area into a paint booth using plastic sheeting. They used an Epoxy paint—and there was no ventilation. Dave used a wet handkerchief while Phil used no mask. Phil ended up in a hospital, where he was told that with only a little more exposure, his lungs would have been severely damaged.

While attending school in St. Paul, the two had lived in an apartment several blocks from campus. I was told that during mid-winter it was necessary for them to wear full face masks and parkas. It seems that the head parka needed to protrude forward from the face in order that one's breath would provide warmth that might keep the eyeball moisture from freezing! Without some such precaution it was possible that the eye itself could freeze.

Fuzz Nichols became CEO of the Washer Service Company. His two sons worked for the Washer end of the company—the repair and maintenance section.

At the time, my mother needed a replacement washer. "No problem," said the boys. They provided a rebuilt machine. It was put to work and lasted for about two weeks. My mother became perturbed and the Nichols were frustrated. It was suggested that we all regroup.

My mother obtained a new machine and the Nichols boys went back to machine repairing.

I never asked how the boys fazed out of the washer repair business, though they did become successful businessmen in Southern California. At the time of this writing, Phil is living the good life on the gold coast, just north of San Diego, and Dave is retired in Texas.

Don Fryklund, Gloucester, Mass. At the starting line of the first heat of Formula E runabout at Mountain Home, Arkansas — APBA Stock Outboard National Championship in 1987.

The 45 CID Evinrude 75 was owned by his brother David, who had just obtained the motor from Dave Hammond OMC Director of Research and Development.

The motor was new — had never been on a transom of a boat. David was reluctant to loan the motor to his brother and advised him not to use a hard hand on the throttle till safe and efficient trim angle was achieved. Don used his brother's hydro propeller and advice.

Ha said, "I hit the starting line at about ½ throttle and squeezed gently. The boat fortunately have me immediate trim information. I never advanced beyond ¾ throttle. The boat made water contact about every 50'-75'. I did not know where the competitors were although I could hear their open pipes. I did not look back —I could only dare to look forward. As I hit the finish line, I looked back where the 2ⁿᵈ boat was first enerting the turn. I won the championship —thanked Dave and told him not to worry about another loan."

"Frankly, the torque, weight and power of the Evinrude 75 make the motor unsuitable for use with our small lightweight boats. I never used the motor again. Sometimes one has to use common sense —that outfit got my total attention — one can hold breath only so long!"

Photo Credit - APBA

What's in a Name?

Shortly after World War II, a new type of commercial truck cab appeared on the street. This new design placed the driver cab over the engine. The vehicle was commonly called a Cab-over.

The winter of '48-'49 was a partially cold one in Southern California and a cavern-like boat shop isn't noted for central heating, so a great deal of time that winter was spent around the hot stove. As a result, we discussed, planned, designed and soon thereafter built what was then a rather novel boat form.

Bill and I brainstormed a hydro which would more effectively counter the front lift encountered on the 3-point hydro design which was then beginning to dominate the Alky division. It would be a number of years until the extended aft plane and larger hydro would be proven. A simple solution of the lift problem was to place driver weight forward. All one had to do was elongate the cockpit and place the driver forward of the usual station point. The idea was to develop a boat that was stable and would ride pretty well transom free.

The "Green Ghost" as it was then called, was a strange looking hull. It had a wide rear plane, long, long cockpit, with the steering wheel about twenty-four inches forward of the sponsons. Results, not appearance, were what we were after.

Pep Hubbell, of Rosemead, CA, engine and parts manufacturer, elected to give the boat a try at the first Marine Stadium regatta in Long Beach during the spring of '49. Sunday morning found Hubbell Limping after Saturday testing, so Dick Sherman, mechanical engineer, was nominated test pilot. Pep, incidentally, thought the boat to be the very roughest riding hull he had ever driven!

Sherman tried the boat briefly with the Pr-65 (class C) prior to the race and was quite enthusiastic. In a good field of boats he hit the first turn in third place and came out in front, to romp home the winner. The sight of a driver steering up front, with sponsons displacing, and transom relatively free, was a new one for spectators on the beach.

The late Bert Ball, a C Service runabout driver and Glendale farm produce freighter, was struck with an inspiration. No doubt his background in truck transportation was the source of his comment, "Look, it's a Cab-Over." Bert Ball is remembered by friends and associates for his many contributions to the sport of boat racing. We must acknowledge his apt designation of a major boat from.

The "Cab-Over," then, is a racing hydro driven from a position forward of the sponsons. The ultimate goal, of course, is a free riding transom. The exceptionally clean-riding inboard three-point racing hydro has been the end result everyone is looking for.

A successful boat of this type presents a very difficult problem to the builder and designer. The very nature of the outboard hydro—weight distribution and weight-to-horsepower ration—does not readily lend itself to such a design. The early Cob-Over was further handicapped because surface propellers for outboards did not come along till after 1950.

The long cockpit, with driver forward, is to get as much weight off the transom as possible. This achieves an immediate result—a transfer of weight forward to the sponsons, and a usual jaw-cracking ride. The redistribution of weight presents new problems not previously encountered. The Cab-Over has a noticeable lack of acceleration due to displacement of the two sponsons at application less than maximum horsepower and top speed.

We discontinued building the Cob-Over when we found that the form is practical only in larger classes, the small horsepower motors simply do not have the power to get the Cab-Over the "hump." A C hull, we found through considerable experience, was a border-line class. To be frank, the Cab-Over was not "commercial" for a professional boat builder.

Still, there have been several successes with the cab-over. Notably, Hugh Entrop of Seattle, who attended one of the 1949 Marine Stadium regattas, saw the original "cab-over." Went home and came up with his "Star-flight" series of boats. His 75H mercury and unique cab-over version subsequently won championships and set world records—and later in combination with OMC raised the outboard kilo record to the then remarkable 125mph.

Pride of the Navy

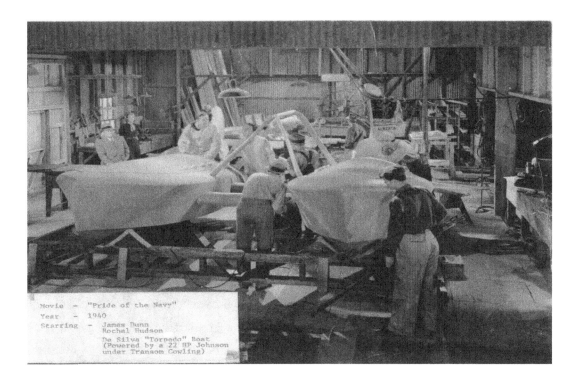

Movie   -   "Pride of the Navy"
Year   -   1940
Starring -   James Dunn
              Rochel Hudson
              De Silva "Torpedo" Boat
              (Powered by a 22 HP Johnson
              under Transom Cowling)

Year: 1938 Republic Studios
Director: Charles Lamont
Cast: Rochelle Hudson, James Dunne, Gordon Oliver, Horace McMann, Gordon Jones

A producer from Republic Motion Picture Studios contracted with John DeSilva in 1938 to design and fabricate a twin hull torpedo boat for a movie to be called "Pride of the Navy".

The movie storyline is of an engineer/sportsman who is hired by the US Navy to design a new type assault weapon. A unique torpedo boat is designed to swiftly approach and destroy a combat ship with their new weapon.

Several weeks were needed to arrive at a design solution then John built two 18' hulls joined with a boom arrangement Similar to a South Sea catamaran) with a torpedo suspended between them.

The photo taken at a Republic Studio set shows the cast working on the nearly completed structure. Note the monkey on James Dunne's back!

Although the movie boat is be powered by a powerful motor within each hull, the boats were actually propelled with a Johnson P-50 on each transom, hidden under a nacelle/fairing. This did not work because of exhaust fumes in the enclosed area, where an engine mechanic was hidden.

(continued) A fast '25 launch was used to tow the structure for the active movie scene. The camera was speeded to make a torpedo boat look like it was going very fast. The scene was short at dusk, so that spectators would not see the cable.

Please, no complaint! This was a B movie and the admission charge was probably only $.75. What do you want for a buck!

The Los Angeles area prior to WWII was the happy stomping and living ground for ordinary people as well as the wealthy. Why not—where else could one get perfect weather, Hollywood, and the casting support?!

My father was also attracted to the area because it was not so adversely affected by the depression, as were other parts of the nation. Southern California was protected from the financial blight through the economic benefit of the aircraft and Movie industries. These two core industries and their necessary infrastructure enabled the area to escape the general malaise.

Movie stars could and would be seen in public with not great attention of surprise. One day we were having lunch at the Farmer's Market, up on 3rd and Sunset, when Steward Granger and his wife Gene Simmons were sitting at the next table. We regularly saw Glenn Ford at marine Stadium, on a weekday, where he had a friend who owned a ski-boat. Once Errol Flynn walked into the Hollycraft boat shop with two huge, white, Afghan dogs on a leash. As they came toward me I asked, "Are those dogs friendly?" The man had dark glasses on and I didn't recognize him until he took them off and said, "Most of the time." Most of us are not inclined to make a public display with two such exotic animals, but Mr. Flynn was probably just living up to his public image.

Another personality, about the same time, showed up at the boat shop. The details are a bit obscure, but my father was hired by Robert Stack to either rebuild or repair an inboard pleasure runabout. Stack was probably six or seven years older than me, and far more sophisticated. I remember him tooling around town in a big convertible—not a hot rod. Shortly thereafter he began to race an Inboard hydroplane, with some success. He campaigned off and on during the War years. Then the movie studio forced him to stop racing due to its hazardous nature. Robert achieved initial notoriety when the nation read, "STACK GIVES DEANNA DURBIN HER FIRST KISS"!

Shortly after the War, Bill and I went to a USC football game at the Coliseum just off Santa Barbara Ave., where we were seated about 50-60 seats above ground level, just off the 50 yard line. We looked around, and just behind us was Ward Bond. Bond made a very successful career as a second fiddle to such stars as John Wayne. Someone asked Bond, "Is this the best seat you could get? Thought you would be on the 50 yard line with the team and John Wayne." (Wayne, whose real name was Marion Morrison, had been a varsity lineman on the SC team prior to becoming an actor.) Bond replied, "this seat isn't bad—I like being with the riff-raff!" Everyone had a laugh.

In late 1937, a man walked into the shop and said, "I'm a producer. We are going to make a movie and need some boat experts to help. The story will be that of a sportsman who has designed a torpedo boat and it trying to sell it to the Navy. We want you to build us a boat."

They wanted a twin hull structure with a torpedo mounted mid-ship. The hulls were meant to look as though they were powered by strong inboards. This was to be a B movie with a limited budget. Most probably the cast took up most of the money—the boat issue was a secondary problem.

The movie folks were not concerned with steering or with figuring out how two substantial hulls were to be joined with integrity, or how a torpedo could be suspended atop the structure.

My father built two rather streamlined (for the time) hulls and attached them via some substantial beans that were heavily disguised. Conical fairings were placed over the P-50 Johnson motor on each transom.

Most of the boat photos were at the studio set, where actors ran around to look like mechanical experts. There is one actual scene in the movie where the boat and actors are on the water. This was at San Pedro, in the inner harbor, where James Dunn is supposed to drive the boat up to a pier, climb out and run a few steps into a landing.

We were on location to see this 3-4 minute scene. The shoot took two days of Dunn repeatedly climbing in and out, walking, stumbling, tripping and saying very little. Rochelle Hudson sat in a cabin cruiser nearby reading and smoking.

Mr. Dunn, at the time, was about 50. He looked good, but was probably in declining years as a leading man movie star. He had been a Broadway song and dance man and had great success in his role with "A Tree Grows in Brooklyn." He had also made a very successful movie with Shirley Temple.

The torpedo boat film was eventually completed and we attended its premiere at a local theatre in 1939. The picture was a moderate success.

There is one scene in the movie where the boat approaches a target at high speed and releases its torpedo. The boat was actually towed by a big powerboat—filmed a dusk when one couldn't see the cable. The camera was sped up so that the torpedo boat looks like it's going very fast.

You can bring up "Pride of the Navy" on the internet and get all the details.

It was the Principle of the Thing

Herb Hadfield was one of my father's first customers when we moved to Southern California in 1937. At that time he was about thirty-five, lived in Culver City and worked for MGM, where he was a chief plumber. He was married, with a son and a daughter.

Herb drove a P-50 powered C service rig. A good friend of Herb Rimlinger, they were often a one-two winner at many regattas.

When World War Two came along in 1941, Herb enlisted in the Army—although he could have avoided service through his family obligations and somewhat defective eyesight. He remained in the service until being discharged in 1945.

Sometime in the early '50's, herb was given a ticket while driving his ten-year old pickup. He asked, "Why are you giving me a ticket, I've certainly not done anything wrong." The cop replied, "You're carrying something in the box of your pickup and you don't have a commercial license."

"I'm not in business and that is only an old lawnmower."

"No matter, you get a ticket."

Herb was appalled at the injustice of the situation. He had a friend who practiced law and asked if there was any solution. Sure enough, the law said that if the hauling vehicles weighs under such-and-such, the commercial license is not required.

Herb went to work, and removed the rear bed, box seats and everything else not needed for the truck to move. He obtained a signed receipt from a certified commercial scale and took it to the local court.

When his case came up, he handed the weight receipt, vehicle law code, and his driver's license to the judge. His honor looked at the data, looked to Herb, smiled and announced, "Case dismissed."

It was the principle of the thing.

In 1776, The American colonies rebelled against injustice and became the United States of America. It's the principle of the thing.

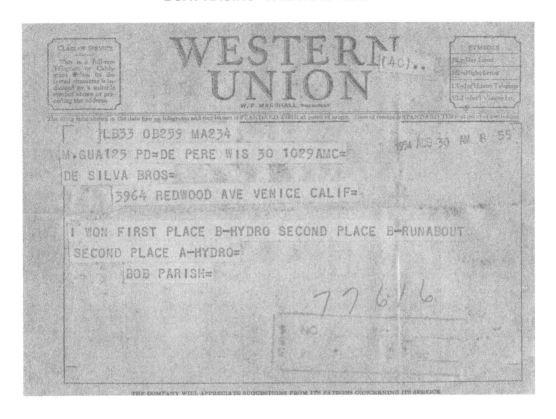

Western Union Telegraph

*"I won first place B-Hydro second place B-Runabout second place A-Hydro
Bob Parish"*

August 30th, 1954

Above- 1968 Lee Sutter
Many knowledgeable outboard racing folks consider Lee Sutter as in one of the top echelon of drivers,
He started in the stock division while in school, Seattle, then graduated to the Alky ranks. He was a contender in everything he drove. Lee and Ron Anderson, Seattle, as a team set many Kilo and competition records in the '60's and '70's. Their national championships were numerous in classes A and B
Lee drove hydros, runabouts and tunnels – his own equipment and that owned by others.
C-82 was a 12' flat deck, powered by an A, 250 CID Konig.
Photo-Swanson

Left- Ralph Donald began his boat racing career in the '50's, when the USA "South" was very active in outboard racing.
Florida with all its water was a natural venue and noise was not the factor it is today.
Donald grew up in the Atlanta area – became a real estate broker with interests in the surrounding area. Because Scott Smith, Dallas, imported the German Konig racing motor and Dallas was but 30 miles away, he tended to favor that brand.
Over a long career, Ralph won more than a normal share of championships. In the 1970's, he started attending races in Europe, where he became well known as a competitor and sportsman.
He drove Alky runabouts till his knees became a problem, then devoted all his activities to the laydown hydro. He also contributed to the sport as an official of the APBA – several as Pro Commission Chairman several times and promoted boat races throughout the South.
He was long associated with the Westbrook racing family of Marietta. Ralph retired as an active driver in 2012 – after a driving career of over 50 years.

Willis Comet

Hot Tomatoe
Blown fuel Chrysler - De Silva hull

1952 Long Beach Marine Stadium

The Hot Tomato hull started out to be just a standard, run-of-the-mill inboard runabout. John DeSilva built the boat on speculation, for inventory.

Eddie Weinberg, LA thought the hull would be ok for the new sport of inboard drag racing; which was becoming popular in Southern California.

Sponsons were added to lessen drag and give punch through the lights. The outfit surprised by attaining the speed of 137+mph and held the speed record for a short time.

Photo-Squires

In 1944 John DeSilva had a stroke which thereafter forced him to retire as an active boat builder.

Bill and I took over the business after World War Two. Since Southern California had been a hotbed of outboard racing prior to the war we felt that a good post-war business could be developed. Harold Rockholt, in Northern California, was the only other established builder. The Phantom built by a man named Shirley did not arrive till after 1950.

Bill attended the 1948 APBA National Outboard Championships at Celina, Tennessee. He was astounded by the large number of Willis "Comet" runabouts, which had had an exsplosive birth just after the war. The Willis Company had built boats prior to the war, but with modest success. The Comet was not a fast boat but sturdily built, could handle rough water, and would turn reasonably well. The large number of Willis boats were not a great concern to us. It meant that the market potential was greater than we had thought, and the Willis Co. specialized in runabouts—the boat form in which we wanted to compete.

We soon determined that the Comet design had a fatal flaw and thought that the brand would quickly become a non-factor. We were mistaken. It took ten years before the Willis Comet became obsolete.

The design problem was that the boat had an excessive up and down bow movement, regardless of water conditions and motor setup. This is not good. Each time the bow comes down markedly, it produces drag on the forward plane and a speed reduction. Each time the bow rises it produces drag resistance. Also, the bow movement does not allow the boat to properly lock-up in the turn, resulting in excess dynamics and loss of speed. In other words, the trim angle is never at a constant— which would reduce speed.

The cause of this excessive bow movement was the boat's bottom transom overhand of perhaps four or five inches. The Willis Co. never did anything to correct their fatal flaw. This may seem odd, but possibly not unusual. Resistance to change is a normal human characteristic. Still, resistance to change in a racing activity does not lead to success.

The Willis brand took hold because the boat was available at a reasonable price, and its performance was acceptable. There had been no professional builder in the East till the Willis arrived, since the West Coast boats took much longer to penetrate the East due to transportation problems, small problems, small productions, and unknown performance. The Willis solved these problems—it was the product that drivers jumped on when they wanted to complement their PR and SC tables.

Follow the Leader

The first boat John DeSilva sold in the Los Angeles area was to Herb Rimlinger. John had built a boat on speculation and brought it down from Stockton to promote some sales in Southern California. He rented some space within a large boat and motor dealership—Holly Craft Marine, on Pico BLVD. in west Los Angeles.

AT that time, in 1936, Herb operated a sheet metal shop on Roberston BLVD. in Culver City. He was also a member of the City council.

Herb had arguably the best P-50 Johnson on the West Coast, as well a pretty good PR-65. He had been driving a locally-built runabout, but was ready for a new boat.

Prior to WWII, the P-50 motor was probably a touch superior to the Evinrude Speeditwin C Service motor. In those days, C Service was a phenomenon in the West Coast runabout scene. The popularity was not due to cost, but to speed, which then was between forty-five and fifty miles per hour: not bad for a fishing motor and two-hundred pound, thirteen-foot long boat. While Northern California and Seattle were largely dominated by Evinrude C Service, it was not till after WWII that the Evinrude potential was recognized, upon which the C Service class expanded with a hydro and became National.

In 1939 a large group of C Service drivers came down to the Hearst Regatta at Long Beach Marine Stadium, which was the venue for many outboard racing events in the 1930's. This particular regatta was one of the Hearst Newspaper extravaganzas—one of the major events on the West Coast. Drivers from as far away as Denver and Idaho often attended.

Contest between the Johnsons P-50 and the Evinrude Speeditwin was at its height. The P-50 may have had a slight edge, a bit more punch. However, the Evinrude had a better lower unit and probably more pure speed.

At this regatta were twenty-two SC runabouts, competing on a fifty yard wide channel around a single buoy turn. Someone made the claim that he could walk across the course over the deck of the twenty-seven 4-60 runabouts entered.

In the first heat of the Service C runabout Lloyd Huse, the thirty-four year old mayor of Yuba City and one of the better Evinrude drivers, got a great start and led into the first turn in his Rockholt boat and Evinrude motor. Alongside him was Herb Rimlinger with his Johnson P-50 and new DeSilva runabout.

The two went around the course for five laps neck-and-neck: Huse on the inside and Rimlinger on his hip. They finished that way—Huse first by a few seconds.

The second heat started the same way. Huse came out of the first in the lead, Herb on his transom. Rimlinger was asked why he got himself into that position in both heats. He replied, "Because of the mass of boats I could not get the position I wanted. I knew that I had to so something unorthodox, else I would end up second."

The two repeated what they had done in the first heat. They went around each turn with Rimlinger on the outside, slightly behind. But on the last turn things changed. Huse went wide, thinking that Herb would do what he had done through the nine turns.

Rimlinger, however, knew Lloyd would do as he had in the first heat—swing wide. Herb instead drove across Lloyd's wake and cut to the inside. Positions were reversed: Rimlinger first, Huse second. Rimlinger won the race by five seconds.

Sometimes garnering a win requires more guile than speed!

Don't Judge a Book by its Cover

Sometime around 1950 a man walked into the shop who showed no indication of what he became in boat racing.

He said, "I'm a farmer-dairyman from Bakersfield who has two young sons and I want them to become involved in boat racing. I'm a widower, and recently had a terrible auto accident which has left me somewhat of a cripple. My oldest son George just graduated from high school and the other is three years younger. Boat racing may be the activity which can keep me close to my boys and keep us all out of trouble. I've heard that you fellows build a good boat—can you help me?"

This was our introduction to Buck Parish, who was then around 62. The auto accident had left him with one hand that was about 60% usable. He was dressed in Farmer's overalls, patched and well worn. He chewed tobacco. You would say he was not worth a second glance. Big mistake. His mind was sharp, he knew what he wanted and he had the drive and determination to get there.

We built the Parish's an A stock Runabout and a hydro. They took their equipment to Hart Memorial Park outside Bakersfield for testing. This was after the school day when activity on the water was quiet. Both boys were only slightly above average height and had slender frames – ideal for the small stock class.

We did not receive any word from the Parish's throughout that first winter and early spring. Then, after one of the early regattas, I received word that someone named Parish had finished high up in the race result.

Now, in the early era of stock racing in Southern California, the interest and activities were huge. In California there were most always elimination heats in order to get to the final. Today entry at some of the better events would be over several hundred. To place in these races was an accomplishment. There was no little sophistication in those early days despite the fact that no one was really expert in the vital components of what makes a planning boat go fast. Raising the motor up and down and change of propellers was, of course, basic. Most west coast stock drivers at that time were dependent upon two propeller sources— the Mercury Kamic and the Oakland Johnson. The Johnson Propeller Co. had been around for many years. I can remember, as a child, going to the Oakland foundry with my father and Ernie Millot. Sometimes they would pick up a number of props and go out to the Estuary, with Oscar Johnson, for testing. Probably, Millot and Mr. Johnson were the experts behind the Johnson racing propeller program. As this is written, the Johnson design propeller is still the prop of choice in the Evinrude C Service Class: 80 Years!

Sure enough, the Parish I knew had done well. Robert quickly became the dominant driver of the Parish team. George was more interested in promoting the family business activities. But Bob was blessed with an athletic body, keen reflexes and good eyesight. He very quickly mastered a driving technique few are able to achieve.

At one Long Beach regatta the Parish's main competition was Elgin gates in B stock runabout. Elgin, at the time, was a veteran driver who had obtained the Southern California distribution for Mercury Motors. All the Kamic propellers were coming through this facility; he had the latest equipment. Elgin also was driving a Phantom style runabout, built in Oregon, which was reported to be very fast.

This photo was taken shortly before 15 year old Bob left to attend the 1954 APBA Stock Nationals at Depere, Wisconsin.

The Championships were dominated by SWIFT Brand Hydros which were extremely popular. Parish had the only off brand boat to win – the A stock hydro class. The DeSilva boat may not have been the fastest, bob reported, but the water was rough and he got good starts – two advantages others could not overcome.

Photo-Hitchcock

Buck told Bobby to start on the inside. He knew that Gates might have superior speed but that his acceleration would probably be a little short. The two boats went into the first turn—a single buoy—side by side. Bob had developed a unique turning style which enabled him to literally spin on a dime. I have seen a good many driving techniques, but Bob Parish was the only driver I have ever seen who was able to turn a boat like that. Our runabout at that time was not a chine turner. The chine turn runabout would not come on the scene for perhaps 10-15 years.

Elgin tried to say with Bob in the turn, but the Phantom was not capable of the Parish maneuver – it flipped. I didn't know till later that Buck had heard that Northern California Mercury distributor had received a new, faster Kamic propeller and had obtained one prior to the race. So he was confident that Gates would not have something better.

The constant testing at Hart Park resulted in a boat and motor setup that proved to be superior for as long as the Parish's continued in boat racing. Long dominate in stock boat racing, in later years they moved to the Alky division, with Quincy-Merc motors. They were not as superior in the Alky division—

probably because Buck's health deteriorated and the two boys were about to become cotton farmers in Australia.

McCulloch

You think boat racing is all sweetness and light—no skullduggery ever goes on—no "my way or the highway"? Here is a true story that may enlighten you. Some names have been omitted, for evident reasons.

The grand episode takes place in the mid '60's', a great time to live in the Los Angeles area. People were doing marvelous things all over town; there was a dynamism in the air. Why not? The weather was super—one could do most anything without regard to the weather. The LA chamber of Commerce, which had worked overtime prior to World War One, was practically moribund because of the postwar population explosion. And, within that population shift was a huge number of talented people.

Our shop in Culver City was surrounded by an ocean of human talent working in big and small business. MGM studios were a few blocks away on Washington Blvd. Douglas Aircraft was going full blast in Santa Monica and was building an even larger facility in Long Beach, just south of San Pedro and its great harbor; Howard Highes had flow his "Spruce Goose" within the harbor after its overland trip from his plant in Playa del Rey. We had purchased tools and lumber from the Hughes surplus store.

The birth of the American Hot Rod vehicle took place in the area. Back in the '30's, it was the passion for every kid for get hold of a Ford Model A, strip it down, get rid of the fenders, heat up the motor, apply some paint or primer, take it to Muroc Dry Beds (near Edwards Air Force Base) and see how fast it would go. Parts and Engine builders, Iskendarian, Moon Edelbrock, Harmon, Black, Eddie Meyers, Merer/Drake Offenhouser, and many others were friends and neighbors.

Indianapolis race cars were nearly all built in LA. They were freighted to Indianapolis by the Flying Tiger Airfreight Co., whose sales rep was a friend who helped ship many race boats until the airfreighters became super-efficient and went to containers, which alienated perhaps twenty percent of their business. The loss was short term—efficiency gradually helped their bottom line.

Major Industry in Southern California was complimented by a terrific source of human talent. And supportive business: a great infrastructure. Regardless of human ability, industry needs all manner of supplies, tools office and floor personnel, and management. Everything was available: doctors, lawyers, food, entertainment and housing.

Young folks and old from throughout the US and abroad came to work, and to study at local schools and universities: SC, UCLA, Pepperdine, Loyola, Occidental, Cal Tech, Art Center, and the wonderful California State College/University system.

Robert McCulloch was one such transplant, whose timing and foresight were excellent. His Origins were in the Eastern USA, but he moved his corporation to Century Blvd. (Across from the early site of the LA airpoirt terminal) when the area was akin to a bean field.

The location became increasingly valuable and was probably the financial source for the soon-to-come development of Site Six. Site Six was a boat landing on the Colorado River above Parker Dam, on the dirt road to Needles. The motor test site and landing eventually became Lake Havasu City.

Prior to his move west, Robert McCulloch had acquired Scott-Atwater Outboard Motor Corporation. His chainsaw manufacturing business was a huge success, and he wanted to build on that success by expanding into outboard motors. It was a perfect fit.

Scott-Atwater was a relatively good acquisition. It had a recognizable name, a decent reputation, and a distribution system with scope for improvement-all in all, good potential. The company also had a modern product line which could be exploited.

The booming years of the '60's were good for the McCulloch Corporation. Their Scott-Atwater venture, though not a true financial success, expanded their horizon and furthered the likelihood of a hopeful future.

For Robert McCulloch's birthday in 1960, some of

Bill Holland, Houston is prepping his McCulloch 590 powered hydro for a test run at a local Houston lake.

Bill was a veteran outboard racing driver, who had campaigned both hydro and runabouts throughout the US with considerable success.

He had obtained a job in Los Angeles with the McCulloch Corporation because of his motor mechanical expertise. Because the McCulloch 590 was a legal class F motor, Bill became fascinated with its potential in organized NOA and APBA racing.

Holland built a special motor for an attempt at a limited CID world record, which at the time was held by equipment assembled at the OMC Evinrude factory.

the senior staff decided to have a hydroplane built and surprise the boss with a racing package at the celebration. He had driven a hydro in in the 1930's while attending one of the Ivy League schools under the banner of the Inter-Collegiate Boat Racing League.

We were selected to build the boat. It was to be Lace Curtain: no expense spared. The contract was our probably because we were located nearby and we had known Robert Kies, a senior McCulloch employee, for some years. He knew boat racing through his own driving and engine expertise.

BOAT RACING - THEN AND NOW

We completed boat #FH126039 in December 12, 1960. We heard that the boat and 590 motor combination was one of the birthday highlights. The boat was one-of-a-kind: oak and mahogany planking, trimmed in Walnut, and finished and polished by the best craftsmen we could find.

Sometime later we were contacted by Bob Kies about campaigning the hydro and a 590 motor at the 1964 APBA Alky National Championship to be held at Casper, Wyoming. We were asked to provide a driver for the equipment, which would be eligible for the F Hydro class. At that time the class was dominated by the 6 cylinder Mercury, often souped up by O.F. Christener of Quincy Welding fame. Also on hand would be the slowly fading Evinrude 4-60 motors in the capable hands of a few die-hards such as Clark (Bud) Wiget, George Mishey, John Taprahanian, Bert Ball, John Mokranin, and a few others. The 4-60 was, in 1964, still a formidable competitor.

Bill Holland, Houston, Texas drives the DeSilva 15' hydro powered by a McCulloch 590, through the NOA Kilo at a speed of 106+mph.

This was a new NOA record. The world record for a limited CID outboard hydro was 112mph so Holland's mark was short of desired speed. The motor Holland had brought for the attempt had broken while testing, so Bill had to borrow a local dealer's motor.

Although disappointed, Holland felt that the effort did establish the fact that the rig had the potential to do better. Time and expense precluded him from making a further effort.

It should be noted that this record attempt was a one-man effort – no help, either technical or financial was given to Bill Holland by the McCulloch Corporation.

The McCulloch corp. had designed a developed a series of large capacity motors. These were necessary for the company to be competitive in the marketplace. The public had enthusiastically adopted the sport of water skiing, an activity that demanded large boats and motors—larger, certainly, than those needed for fishing or hunting. The major outboard manufacturers were not long in providing more powerful and convenience. McCulloch Corp., to be a factor in the industry, had to keep pace.

The three cylinders, 60 HP Flying Scott, which was lifted to 75HP in 1961, was the result. From this power head, McCulloch designed the 590 and 630 motors. They were 59 and 63 inches of displacement; both large bore and short stroke. The 630 had the Flying Scott bore and stroke, while the 590's stroke was

105

slightly shorter. Their reed valves were replaced with cylindrical rotary valve, and an intermediate set o gears above the lower unit allowed for ratio changes in ten percent increments from 1:1 up to 2:1. This adjustability allowed the choice of an efficient propeller/rpm combination for different boats and speeds.

The company had been able to prove these new racing motors by competing in the new form of boat activity—Marathon racing. Such events, over long distances, for a number of hours, by large numbers of boats, are formidable, hazardous, and demanding of participants and equipment.

All forms of boats were used in marathons—deep V and flat bottom runabouts, and the new design tunnel. Two, three, four and five engine boats were on the water.

The 590 McCulloch engine had never participated in Alky outboard racing. Would the motor be viable against the powerful, high winding Alky's? Bob Kies reported that the company knew their motor would be an under-dog, but they were interested in its potential and wanted to uncover its shortcomings.

We were able to obtain Harry Bartolomei as driver for the McCulloch equipment. The factory would provide crew and back-up needed for the project, including fuel, propellers, and manpower. Bartolomei later reported that insufficient time was given to on-the-water testing at Casper. It took considerable time for the factory team to work out a reasonable gear ratio to match their propellers.

Harry's speed was somewhat short, but with the 590 his acceleration and control were excellent. He was able to go through the turns faster than the Merc's and about as fast as the 4-60's. His starts in the two heats of the championship finals were good, and he ended up placing overall third—a rather remarkable achievement for a first time effort, with equipment untried, unproven, and virtually untested.

The motor probably had limitations with Alky outboard racing. It was not a high rpm motor, had a huge amount of torque and was heavy. This combination was okay for large substantial speed boats, but not ideal for a small, light-weight hydro. McCulloch was pleased with the Casper National attempt but chose not to proceed with further such activity.

During the '60's we built a number of highly specialized boats for the McCulloch corporation. One was a small 3-pt. hydro, used as a platform for one of their small motors, placed inboard, with a drive through the bottom into a lower unit. Robert McCulloch's son was responsible for that project. We never heard the conclusion of that effort, although it did seem promising. The project probably failed because of steering and prop shaft angle considerations.

We also built a 20', twin engine, 3-pt. wing hydroplane to demonstrate the 590 and 630 racing motors at various boat shows within the USA. The boat was used for one demonstrating season, then was retired. The boat then participated in a Colorado River marathon, in Parker, Arizona. Unfortunately, the engines failed shortly after the start.

Sometime later we had occasion to visit the Century BLVD. research center and see them working on several boat rigs which were to be raced in Paris at the six hour marathon to be held that fall. Great!

But, as we looked at the equipment, it occurred to us that it didn't look right.

BOAT RACING - THEN AND NOW

I had attended the Paris Marathon in 1956 and 1966. The Seine River flows through Paris, creating the right and left banks. In the middle of the river the Cite—the little island site of Notre Dame Cathedral.

The Six Hour Marathon was usually sited west of the Cite, several bridges down, near the Eifel Tower. For those who have not been to Paris and have not looked at the Seine as it flows through town, it should be known that this is no safe venue for a boat race—for a number of reasons, all related to its hazards.

The river is banked on each side with Vertical Brick and concrete walls, sometimes twenty feet high. Approximately every quarter mile a bridge crosses the river, each with an abatement protruding into the river for 10-15 feet. River barges park along the numerous quays. Commercial and pleasure boats constantly move about. Some of the river traffic is curtailed during the race, but not all! It would probably take a de Gaulle to stop the French from establishing monetary effort!

The race course is about 3 kilos long. Spectators view the race from both river banks and bridges. After 50-75 or more runabouts, tunnels, hydroplanes, inboards and outboards, single and twin engine boats start this event, one can visualize the horrendous water conditions.

A number of large shallow barges are used as the pit area. The French officials place their conducting committee on the opposite, right bank—where they perhaps are shielded from any irate competitors.

T-65 was the first twin engine boat built by the DeSilva brothers.

Tom Roath, Denver Boat & Motor dealer, had two new 4 cylinder Evinrude motors and asked us to build him a boat for the upcoming Havasu City Marathon.

We had been to the 6 hour Paris Marathon in 1966 and had some idea as to a boat needed for the Colorado River event. The boat was to be a pure tunnel with the engine mounted on each sponson. We knew speed and punch were to be important, for boats from all over the US and Europe were to be competitors. At the same time, water conditions would certainly be a factor on the 6 mile course—with a dog-leg on one end and a sweeping 3 buoy on the other.

In 1966, Paris, the Molinari's were vastly superior and most like the same would be true on the Colorado.

Two hours into the first day found Tom Roath in first place. When he came into the puts for fuel, jack Leek, OMC racing manager, invited him to fuel at the factory pump— rather than use tom's hand operation by his pit crew. At the end of the first day, 4 hours, Tom was race leader.

The boat proved to be very capable in coping with race conditions. The back straight proved to be long and at times quite rough – Tom glided over that quite well. One turn had a sweeping multiple buoys where the boat passed many of his competitors. He was able to negotiate the dog-leg with no trouble. At the end of the day, a careful check downed no evident problems.

Day two, Tom again led for about 2 hours, when one battery failed. Time in the pits to find the problem – then to replace, pushed tom back to about 7th. In the remaining time, he picked off enough boats to place and overall 4th.

We were delighted with the effort, as was Roath. To meet and beat the best is a satisfactory outcome – in any endeavor.

BOAT RACING - THEN AND NOW

In order to compete under these conditions it is necessary to have specialized equipment. In 1966, we saw the Molinari boats perform. They had designed a tunnel boat for the race. The boat was a 17', twin engine deep tunnel, with high angle sponsons. With those deep V Sponsons, the boat would glide through the water. Ideal for the course!

The OMC factory racing division had, a few years previously, contracted an exclusive with Molinari. This left the Mercury out in the cold! Is Molinari the only good builder of racing craft in the world? No matter, OMC has it, and we want in!

No problem. Italian talent can solve the problem. There is a very talented Molinari cousin who can set up shop nearby—it may not come out of the same door, but who will know the difference?!

The McCulloch team had two Mullins type boats. The Mullins was the prototype design for the later true tunnel race boats. It had appeared in the early '30's. The boat had a spoon bow and a tunnel bottom that ended at the transom water line. The tunnel width at the transom was quite narrow.

The McCulloch boat were similar in design, except that the tunnel depth at transom was about 6" above the water line, and the sponsons were relatively flat. These boats had performed well at the West Coast races, where the water conditions were reasonable.

When we explained things to the McCulloch crew they advised that we talk to G.C. Robechaud, Vice President of Advanced Development Division, who was boss of boat racing. After some discussion, he thanked us for our interest and advice, and said that he was confident that their effort was a good one—he had been to Paris and knew the city. Polite, but we'll do things my way!

Now things get interesting. The following is a personal report of a Belgian boat driver whom we had long known. He was visiting his mother in Lille at the time, and knew some of the individuals involved.

The McCulloch boats arrived in Belgium and were stored in the Antwerp McCulloch warehouse, awaiting the trip to Paris. Now, if you are a large Paris boat builder and competitor, you might suppose that an American company would come to a major European regatta with nothing but the best and latest in boat design. Right? That being the situation, get our Belgium friends and send up a crew to look at and measure these American boats.

So it was done. Through friends of friends the warehouse was opened and a three man team spent several hours after midnight inspecting the two boats. First they were somewhat surprised that the boats did not appear to be of advanced design—in fact, they looked plebian. No matter, this was American stuff! We'll take photos and measurements, and analyze later.

A short time later water conditions were as they always will be—awful. The McCulloch boats lasted through the first half hour and then retired due to major problems. The Molinari hulls won the race. American prestige took a nose dive, and the McCulloch team returned home with no fanfare—just sadness and wisdom.

As some Greek or Roman said, "If one does not know the lessons of history, one is condemned to repeat history's errors."

1954 Salton Sea California

99Y-Lou Kay, was built in 1953 at our shop in Mar Vista, California.

Dale Drake, Sonny Meyer and Doc Ingalls all had an input on the redesign of the plan given to us. The boat was on interesting project and a challenge, for we had not previously made a racing inboard hydro. Its material and superstructure were a bit different than on the usual outboard boat.

Anything powered by a Meyer/Drake Offenhauser built motor had to be first rate, so the boat's future was bright.

The proved to be so, for Sonny Meyer drove the boat very successfully for a few years before going to other racing activities.

The world record at Salton Sea in 1954 was but one great race. The boat has had many owner's and drivers over ther years – and has had a very long career.

We only built one Lou-Kay, 48 CID inboard hydro.

Photo-Hitchcock

1961 – McAlester, Oklahoma

Lowell Haberman, Reseda, California is the proud owner of the equipment Dale Kaus, Minnesota has just driven to the B Runabout NOA National Championship.

Dale was well acquainted with the British Anzani motor. He had won several championships while driving for Bill Tenney, the American Anzani importer.

Dale won his first NOA National Championship at Springfield, Illinois where he won with Bill Tenney's B Anzani powered hydro in 1959

The Anomaly

Is motor setup important? Indeed it is—it's critical and can be the ball game.

We encountered a problem during the latter part of the 70's, when we faced a game changing anomaly. We had sold a runabout to Don Nichols, of the Texas/Louisiana part of the country. He attended the APBA Alky nationals in San Antonio in 1978, where he told us that he was having problems with the boat. The boat was checked thoroughly and nothing was found that could or should have produced the problems described.

We took the boat back to California for a complete physical—and found nothing adverse! Then we brought it to a race at Bakersfield where we had Fred Hauenstein drive it around the course for our observation and his reaction. The boat was set up normally. Water conditions were okay, so we were confident that some solution would be found.

Fred ran around the course several times. When asked his reaction to performance, he replied, "The boat is great, build one for me just like it!"

Now we had a problem. We had two fine drivers who had opposite reactions to the same boat!

We then did something that had often been overlooked. We checked motor setup on the boat, the propeller used, and everything that could possibly affect performance.

Hauestein had installed his motor according to normal West Coast method: Prop shaft slightly out from parallel with the bottom, with body weight placed over or just forward of the bubble. His propeller had some rake.

A check with Nichols and several other Eastern drivers indicated that they were setting Eastern style: prop shaft angle was under from parallel, with body weight over or a bit back of the bubble. Their propellers had little or no rake (Hydro style).

The Eastern motor setup tended to make a runabout ride flat, with a tendency to spin in turns.

Our solution was to change the runabout planning surface so that either setup method would be satisfactory. This was not an easily solved problem. Fortunately, the advent of the runabout side fin arrived and helped the turn problem.

However, we still found it necessary to advise each customer of the pros and cons of motor setup and propeller usage.

Most drivers of experience prefer a boat that tells them what it wants to do—then they can react. Currently, a good many drivers seem to like the non-talk boat, which is stable at present speeds, so long as the boat performs reasonably well.

The use of deck design for stability—down pressure—has been a positive help. The conical deck design of the KR was, by the latter '70's, insufficient to stabilize the ever increasing Alky boat speed.

BOAT RACING - THEN AND NOW

We were hesitant to use deck design to increase down pressure; we thought that the bottom could also do so. As this is written, gravitational stability via bottom design is a proven fact, but is probably not something that will be adopted by those who can find down pressure through more normal design.

Still, as V.B. Koriagin said, "Beyond a certain point there is no progress—everything goes downhill!"

1961 Robert Hawie New Jersey

Bob Hawie was a prominent member of the Hawie outboard racing clan. He was assisted by Richard Hawie and R.C. Hawie came along later.

Bob Hawie journeyed to the APBA Stock Nationals – Northern California in 1961 where he won first place in B runabout. He was National Champion till the motor inspector told him his carburetor, although an approved Mercury factory part, had not been approved by the APBA and therefore his motor was not legal.

There was some debate and discussion about the matter but his effort ended all for naught.

R.C. Hawie began boat racing at an early age and when through the ranks of stock, modified and pro (Alky) division racing where he soon attained an enviable record.

Photo-Ted Koopman

Command Pilot

Burnham B. "Bud" Cowdry walked into our shop in the late '50's. A major in the U.S. Air Force, he had come from a posting in the East to a job as liaison with the Rand Corporation in the Venice area.

The Rand Corporation is a world class think tank filled with scholars, scientists, and more PhD than any large university. The Air Force has an on-going contract with the company to study and advise on current and future problems, trends and contingencies the U.S. may experience. Over the years we had some knowledge of the Rand Co. because their facility was nearby and personnel lived in the area.

Bud had been racing some Stock division equipment which he drove for a while without much success, However, he became popular because of a pleasant personality. Everyone liked him and his wife Maggie. After a time he switched from the Stock equipment into Alky boats, buying a C Service runabout and hydro powered with an Evinrude. This was a wise move because the minimum weight in C Service and its gear ratio coped more favorably with his body weight of 250 lbs.

It did not take long for him to have Tom Newton work on his motors. He also got hold of some Gausti/Cary/Radice propellers. We sold him a super light runabout, and Bud Cowdry became a force in the C Service class.

Over a long period of time, we have known a number of drivers who could be called great starters. None of them were better at starting a boat race than Cowdry. His approach to most problems was analytical. He knew that if one got to the first turn in first place, the chance of winning the race was better than good. Over many years and many boat races, we *never* saw him cross the starting line other than in first or second place—legally.

We always sold him light boats with a little more bottom width to hold his weight, so that it was not the handicap it otherwise might have been.

Cowdry retired from the Air Force as a Lt. Colonel and remained in Southern California until he accepted a job as ROTC Commander at a school in Birmingham, Alabama. Bud was not fond of Alabama because boat racing there was almost non-existent. We lost track of him for a while—he moved around a good bit—but then ran into him in Lakeland, Florida. He and Maggie had purchased a property on one of the Florida grand canals. He palled around with a 14' alligator and acted as a real estate agent in his spare time.

Of course he had an outboard pleasure boat and terrorized the local fish population.

A few things may be said of Lt. Col. Cowdry not known to many—about his career as an Air Force pilot.

During the war, a much younger, slimmer Cowdry became a pilot after graduating from one of the Ivy League Colleges. He became a Command pilot, one who qualifies as a one, two, three, or four engine

114

pilot. In other words he flew a P-47 fighter, a twin engine B-25 and B-26, whatever three engine aircraft the Air Force had, and the four engine B-17 and B-24 bombers.

During the later war stage he was seconded to the CBI (Chine, Burma, India) theatre and flew missions over the Hump. From the India-Burma border, over the Himalaya mountain range into southern China—probably the most hazardous terrain on earth. This was a 1500 mile route over an incredibly mountainous area where, should the Boeing DC-3 go down, death was certain. No attempt was to be made should a plane down; it was assumed that there would be no survivors.

It was in the CBI that Bud met Maggie who was a nurse in uniform. After the war, he stayed in the service. He was a command officer, the pay was tolerable, life was good. It did not take long for the Air Force to make him a Lt. Colonel. The rest is history.

Racie

His name was Ray C. Harris. We, of course, called him Racie.

Born about 1915 in Michigan, he avoided poverty during the depression by working in Detroit with one of the major auto manufacturers.

Prior to World War Two he moved to the San Francisco Bay area where GM had a large plant. At the same time he joined the California National Guard. He said, "I joined for patriotic reasons and also thought a war was coming." Perhaps—but there were also economic reasons. They paid per diem while on duty, and he got to wear a fancy uniform.

We have encountered many fascinating personalities within boat racing; Ray Harris was right up there. On one day you would think, "I've got him figured"—and the next day he would astound with a new quirk. One could label him accident prone. Over the period of many years he was involved in a number of incidents.

We sold him one of the first cab-over hydros, which he powered with a 4-60 pumper.

During a heat at Canyon Lake, Arizona, he lost control and fell out of the boat. The automatic throttle did not automate and the boat took off across the lake at what appeared to be full throttle directly into the canyon cliff.

Some time prior he was testing before the start of the program at Long Beach marina Stadium when the carburetor locked coming into the pits. His speed was probably 50-60 mph at the time. Rather than run up into the beach and create havoc, he purposely pulled the boat over. This of course, stopped the boat, but at the price of a blown powerhead.

The Mercury KG-9 was introduced sometime around 1950. Racie decided to get one and had us build a runabout in order to attend the upcoming Stock Nationals in Texas.

We were told by the West Coast Mercury distributor, Elgin Gates, that the KG-9 was a fantastic piece of machinery—"it would provide more power than a 4-60, with a lot fewer cubic inches! Build a big boat for it!"

We decided to build a 14' double cockpit which would weight around 175lbs. The boat was completed with no time for testing. Racie would test at the Nationals.

To make a long, sad story short, the KG-9 effort at the Texas Nationals ended up being too much boat and excessive weight. The motor was a disappointment—Ray sold the boat and the motor, which went to Ed Craven who had us build a 12' runabout. This combination went on to achieve good success in the DU class for the next several years.

During WWII, Ray's guard unit was incorporated into the Army's field artillery. Early on he was stationed on the big island of Hawaii, where he was tasked with surveying training. Never one to flunk and operative request, he got the job done. He found that at a prior time, a similar survey had been completed and was available for comparison.

He ended up on the island of Luzon in the Philippines. While scouting in advance of his unit, in a jeep, he encountered a Japanese squad in a nearby wood. Ray spotted some enemy soldiers in a copse and stood up in the jeep to get a shot at them with his Colt.45.

After he'd unloaded the pistol a mortar round hit the jeep. Ray said the vehicle was shattered and the toes of his right foot were mangled. He was evacuated home and shortly thereafter became a civilian. He received a disability pension for the rest of his life. While going through therapy at the Las Vegas Rehabilitation center he met his wife, Laura. They arrived in the Los Angeles area in 1947, where he opened an upholstery shop.

1952 Salton Sea, California

Ray Harris, Culver City, is driving the 4th cab-over ever built. It was a 12'6", 4:60 powered hull. The motor had been streamlined by a sheet-metal expert, who worked for one of the local movie studios.

The pumper motor broke a crankshaft which destroyed the crankcase and racked one of the cylinders. Ray gave up the Alky F class hydro and continued racing with a runabout.

The saga of Ray Harris is told in another part of this book.

Photo-Hitchcock

At about age fifty, he began to have a problem with arthritis. His hands increasingly refused to function properly, and he had to give up his occupation. For the rest of his life he had no formal way of making a living. But he now found time for the things he loved to do.

By instinct Ray was a gambler. He loved going to the track. He became a regular at Santa Anita, Hollywood Park, Del Mar and the track at Tia Juana, Mexico.

He probably lost more than he ever gained. But it's all in the game—right? He walked into the shop one day and waved a piece of paper at us: "This is my house mortgage—I just paid off the loan with what I won at Hollywood Park!"

He went to the Klamath River one fishing season and became hooked on the sport, even becoming a Rogue River fishing guide. Although we specialized in building race boats, Ray prevailed on us to build him a series of special river-fishing boats: oak framing, half-inch 5 ply planking, twin seats with compartments and super-strong transom! We eventually built four of these boats—all of which he eventually sold for a ton of money. They're probably going strong today.

Ray Harris became more than a customer—he became a friend. Because he had no formal occupation in the latter part of his life, he was often in our shop. He was not a distraction, not in the way; he just hung around.

Laura, his wife, contracted Lou Gehig's disease. A good part of Ray's time and energy was taking care of her. He turned his home into a medical care effort.

Despite the multitude of his personal problems, Ray never gave in to despair. On the contrary, his general attitude was that "Life is a blast you only have one go around, and may as well enjoy it!"

Multi-talented, Ray Harris could do almost anything. He was a self-taught machinist, a hypnotist, comedian, magician, surveyor, upholsterer, bartender, and gambler. He was a go-to person. "I can't do it" was not in his vocabulary.

The Duel

Two drivers take center stage in this episode. Bill Tenney and Orlando Torigiani.

Anticipation is perhaps the foremost emotion you experience when attending a big race event, and one of our great anticipations in those days was what Bill Tenney would dream up to gain an edge on his competition. Everyone wants to win—but some more than others. And there are those who put more into the effort than time and money. Tenney always seemed to have an edge. Of course, he had the financial means to have the best mechanical equipment—motors and boat propellers. He also had another resource: a creative mind. He did not have a formal mechanical background, though his higher education had been in arts at Yale, but, he had a terrific informal mechanical education.

He had grown up among some of the creative, self-sufficient mechanical folks in America: the lumber industry. His father had been a major lumber figure in Minnesota. In 1935, Bill's father thought it prudent to ship the prodigal son to "season" on the family timber interests in Oregon, where he would be unlikely to get into any serious scrapes. This occurred after Bill had started driving outboards in the East.

My first exposure to Tenney was in 1935 a Long Beach marine Stadium. Bill and a few friends arrived at the stadium with a big auto towing a makeshift trailer filled with boats and motors. One of these boats caused a mild sensation. It looked like an over-sized bathtub, with a 2-6 extended out to thirteen feet. He called this hydro of uncertain origin a runabout! In those days a runabout was a boat of definite size and description; tradition and measurements were clearly applicable.

Although of some amusement to me, the sight outraged my father and most of responsible participants. Most of the morning on race day was spent arguing whether Tenney's boat would be allowed to run. The official decision was to flat outlaw the "thing."

Bill did manage to put the contraption into the water while the controversy raged. Many years later after becoming acquainted with this remarkable personality, we realized that he probably knew first hand that the "runabout" (Boom) would not be allowed to compete—he merely wanted to "rock the boat" and tweak the establishment. After all, a 20 year old kid had to have some fun!

Bill Tenney

Bill drove both Neal (Above) and Fillinger Hydros.

The boat above is a "Banjo" model, with a PR-56 Johnson motor.

At this time Bill lived in Dayton, Ohio.

In 1957, The NOA and APBA Alky Nationals were one week apart. The NOA regatta took place on the bank of the Wabash River near Mt. Carmel, IL; McKeesport, Pennsylvania was the venue for the APBA regatta.

(I should say something about the Monongahela River area near and around Pittsburgh. Rich farmland and timberland surrounded the country till coal was discovered in 1760. One-fifth of the US steelmaking capacity was then concentrated in the area. The flow from row upon row of furnaces along the river lit up the sky for miles. Sooty, dirty air hung everywhere. Trees, streets, houses were covered with a black smoke pall. The river appeared to be a sewer filled with debris and garbage. All in all, not a place one would choose for habitation.)

Claude Fox promoted the NOA regatta, and it was a big one. This was the era when the PR, KR and Elto SC were still king, through the Konig and Christner Merc had appeared on the scene.

For several years, a number of drivers had attained top flight status in each class and competition was

The Ingalls' C Hydro, in the early '50's was about as hot an outfit as one could find.

In 1966, he won the first heat of the C with his PR-65, at the Long Beach Marine Stadium APBA Outboard Championship Regatta – against the legendary equipment of such competition as that of Jack Maypole, Bill Tenney, Harry Marioneau, Bud Wiget, Rocky Stone, Doug Creech, Bill Schuyler and a few others. An ignition problem came up in the second heat.

That was to be his swan song for he retired shortly thereafter to devote his time and effort to the dental profession.

keen, but none more so than the KR, A class hydro. Tenney, Paul Kalb, Orlando Torigiani, Tom Ingalls, Gil Peterman and several others were all possible winners in that class.

Torigiani probably had the best motor. Of Button Willow, California, Orlando was a well-to-do cotton grower. A large group of Italians had immigrated to the lower San Joaquin Valley and created a cotton farm belt west of Bakersfield. Orlando farmed several thousand acres of prime, flat, productive land and during the summer had nothing to do but water the ground and produce additional wealth. This gave him and his cousin Elmo Bellomini enough spare time to race boats. Orlando was an outstanding self-taught machinist and had all the essential machinery to do whatever was required. He had been interested in boat racing prior to WWII but had devoted those years to his family interest. After the war he had time to pursue his competitive spirit.

Tenney arrived at the NOA with a Walt Blankenstein built, very modified Johnson KR class A motor, a new Fillinger boat and Smith props. But would that be enough? Probably not. He had raced against all the competitors and knew that he was not superior.

The Johnson KR lower unit was not something that induced admiration. After all, the motor had been designed around 1930 and the lower unit was not a streamlined beauty. So Bill had replaced the factory lower unit with a much more streamlined Champion unit. In order to do this, it had been necessary to reverse the polarity of the motor. We knew that this was possible to do with a two-cycle motor, but I had never seen it done. This, of course, had required a different propeller, a different cranking plate, and considerable testing to arrive at an efficient use of the new factors.

And the result was excellent. Bill won the A hydro class by placing first each heat; Orlando Torigiani was second each heat. Prior to the race, consensus among the experts was that Orlando was the likely winner. For a year or two, he had put together and outstanding A hydro outfit. However, Bill Tenney won the Championship and also received plaudits for his remarkable innovation.

What happened after the Mt. Carmel race was extraordinary. We all headed for McKeesport, PA for the APBA Nationals to be held the next weekend. Tenny, of course, felt he had the APBA Nationals locked because had without doubt broken the competition at Mr. Carmel, and the competition here, after all, would be the same group.

Meanwhile, Elmo drove their equipment to Pennsylvania and Orlando flew home. He somehow obtained a champion lower unit, made the necessary adapters, reversed the motor rotation, fashioned a new cranking plate, and found several propellers that seemed right. He then flew East and arrived at McKeesport on Friday morning, with elimination heats to start immediately. Both Tenney and Orlando qualified for the final championship heats.

There seems to be some question as to who won the A hydro championship. My memory is that Orlando did. Of one thing I am certain: Orlando Torigiani beat Bill Tenney. Bill was devastated. He later exclaimed, "I can't believe this. I spent a whole year developing, testing and making this thing work. Torigiani comes along, steals my idea, and beats me—all in one week!"

1956 Mt. Carmel, Illinois NOA Nationals

Left to Right: Bob McGinty, Harry Marioneasux

Louisiana is known for many things. That Alan Smith Bob McGinty and Harry Marioneaux were native can contribute to its flow. Harry, a Prominent oil man owned a first class outboard racing outfit and McGinty was more than able to do it justice.

The Trouble with Harry

Over a race boat building career of many years you are certain to encounter a number of talented folks. It took awhile for the talent of Harry Bartolmei to become evident. Late in the '50's we began to hear of a new driver in Northern California who was notorious for going on his head and doing otherwise spectacular things.

He had a Hal Kelly Wetback (or Airborne) runabout and a Champion Hot Rod motor on the transom. That runabout was designed for use in th Stock Outboard Division—and would be difficult for use with an Alky motor.

Someone advised Harry to get one of our boats. He took a delivery and began testing at the nearby Oakland airport, in its estuary alongside. One morning he phone and said, "Something is wrong. I can't get any speed out of your boat: it's about two mph slower than the Kelly!"

We told him not to expect a top speed reading with our boat. "It's competition boat, not a Kilo design. You should setup in a comfortable manner and you will be fine." It took several boat races to convince Harry that we were right, but gradually he began to win consistently and convincingly. He phoned after several races, admitting, "it's hard to believe, but I'm beating everyone with a speed that seems slow. However, I can really turn this boat and it is great in rough water."

At this time Harry was working in San Francisco as chief electrical engineer for Golden West Broadcasters Radio Station—an enterprise owned by Gene Autry, the famed signing cowboy. On the side, Harry was a self-made mechanic expert and propeller man. He said that he would come South of Chowchilla, where a race was to be held at the local fairgrounds. The little San Joaquin valley town had a good-size man-made lake within the site and he wanted to check out the Southern boat drivers. We told him that his entry would be appreciated but that he should not expect the competition to be easy.

Bob Parish was entered. He was a young high school boy, but he had a very good Mere and knew how to drive a runabout. Several other formidable drivers were also present.

At this race Harry discovered that his Champion motor was not really competitive with Quincy, Anzani, or Konig. Shortly thereafter he bought an Anzani B motor and used it for a short time with good results. Then he phoned and informed us that he had made a deal with Scott Smith in Georgia to represent the Konig racing motor on the West Coast.

Afterword Harry Bartolomei rose to the very top rank of the Alky boat racing. The road had not been easy. It had taken time, effort, and treasure. Few outside his immediate circle knew that he tested two and three times per week at the Oakland estuary, which was sited next to the Oakland airport, where noise was not a factor—even at 6:00am. Harry would rise before dawn, be at the beach around 6-7am, and test for a short period. Then take the equipment home, shower, dress, and be at work around 9:00. After a full shift, he'd head home to spend several hours in the work shop.

BOAT RACING - THEN AND NOW

In 1967 he went to a regatta at San Diego Mission Bay; I drove down with him. He wanted to run on the 1-2/3 mile record course. The event was for inboards, but a few classes of outboards were invited. Harry brought his D runabout and Konig 70cc. The boat was our flat deck design which we had been building since 1954.

San Diego has what is popularly acknowledged the perfect climate and the weather for the race was no exception. Very slight breeze, mild temperatures, and a nice water ripple. Perfect for boat racing. There were only five D runabouts on hand— nothing to compete with Harry—and he won each heat with a huge lead.

To be sure, the Inboards put on a grand show. The big 266 CID hydros were a thunderous, crowd pleasing spectacle. There were the little Ford powered hydros and the huge CID SK runabouts. Most of the Inboard classes were capable of speed well beyond 100mph; the 266 could go beyond 150mph.

As we were all packing to leave, the announcement was made that Harry had a set of

1967 Man Power

This photo will explain why the use of boat cart was introduced.

Lifting 500 lbs of racing equipment in and out of the water many times during testing an race day is and was a chore for even the strongest and most enthusiastic pit men.

We introduced lifting rails on the chine of Alky runabouts in 1963. This made it easier to lift the boat in the pits and to facilitate starting the outboard motor. It was harder to start a motor with the propeller in the water. A pull against compression is a little easier when the prop is out of the water.

Photo: left— crewmember
Walter Johnson
Jim Johnson, Crewman.

new competition record. Everyone was delighted. Then Cam Harmon, Inboard Race Chairman for the day, walked up and said, "They did not announce this over the loud speaker, probably because it was embarrassing, but your D outboard runabout went around the course in a faster time than all the Inboard classes but one—and that was the 266 Hydro"(266 CID and about 400HP).

We had just completed building Harmon an experimental 48 CID Inboard hydro, and he thought we would be pleased that harry had done the course with an Outboard runabout powered by a motor of vastly less horsepower, in better time than Inboard hydros and runabouts capable of speeds far beyond 100 mph. Needless to say, the trip home was a pleasant one!

When chastised for lack of courtesy to fellow competitors by not reducing a margin of victory, Harry often replied, "I'm just trying to get the best out of my equipment, for when I get to the nationals there will probably be someone who will be as fast." He had a valid point; in all his years of boat racing the one man he was unable to beat was Jerry Waldman. Jerry always had the advantage when they competed in a hydro class.

Homer Kincaid, Carbin Cliff, Illinois, awaits a boat weigh-in at the APBA Alky Nationals.

Homer often drove equipment owned by others. There was no one better to place good equipment in the winners circle.

It was often said that anyone who discounted Homer as a competitor, was a fool. He was a metallurgist by trade, a politician by accident (Mayor of Carbin Cliff) and a boat race driver by choice.

He, for many years, was chairman of the APBA alky commission and he was the man from whom the KR runabout was named.

Harry begged, "Please come up with a hydro I can use to beat Waldman!" Our reply was that the runabout was our forte, and a superior hydro at any given time would take too much time and effort. We told him that the hydro had too many basic problems and that solving them was not economical. And, this was a question of change, and change is not easily accepted. Someone once stated that change will be fought by all who standing to lose, as well as the half who benefit, because they are afraid of change.

Some may have resented Bartolomei's success. Perhaps they were frustrated competitors. Still, his fate fell upon other drivers. Homer Kincaid was not entirely appreciated—he won too much! It was said that Homor had on several occasions won every event on the race schedule. We all remember Homer's A-B runabout, a smoking ruin, lying in the corn field outside the La Salle-Peru, Illinois Holiday Inn. To this day the villain and the reason remain unknown.

The Quincy welding team had the same problem. Bill Tenney was resented because he had money and won too often. Bud Wiget was frowned upon because he was a big winner. Many, perhaps, did not know that he raced for seven years before winning his first boat race. It took that long to learn how, and to have enough treasure to put a winning effort together.

In 1983 Bartolomei was the first to establish a kilo record over 100mph in a limited horsepower/CID motor: 102.004 mph with his 13'6 KR runabout powered by a class D Alky (40 CID) Konig Motor. Harry officiated at many local regattas and became chairman of the APBA Pro Division, for a time, in the 1980's. He represented the US in several European would championships and sponsored an Italian team which competed at several world championships held in the US. He spoke fluent Italian and sent his son to Italy for some education.

Harry retired from boat racing soon after the turn of the century. One day he started cleaning some pistols when one accidentally discharged and fatally struck him. It is hard for all who knew him to accept the loss of a great friend through such a mishap.

1960 Florida

Bud Wiget moved to Florida. He also took all of his racing equipment – among which was his 1961 flat deck runabout.
The photo was taken at Lake Hollingsworth – downtown Lakeland.
Except for the occasional Newton powered boat, Bud had the C Service class dominated.
His boat racing career had started with a C Service motor and except for "baby" his Evinrude C racing 6 stud, Bud loved the C Service Evinrude motor and was a master at making it achieve its maximum potential.

I Forgot to Duck

I was called upon to referee a regatta on the Colorado River between Parker Davis and Havasu City in 1964. I don't remember who the race chairman was but he fell down on the job because nothing had been done to setup the race prior to my arrival. No course laid, no buoys, no officials for the judges stand and no timing system. This was supposed to be a premier regatta—one created to set records on the surveyed course.

After much frantic to-do the race was started on Saturday and things went well till mid-afternoon when Bill Boyes came running up to the judges stand and said, "There is a fight in the pits—between Bill Rucker and Harry Bartolomei." Serious stuff! I hurried to the scuffle and found Bartolomie on the ground nursing a bloody nose. There was some shouting and milling about so I asked Rocky Stone to escort Harry back to the pit area and to everyone to calm down. An investigation discovered that two hydros had collided going to the first turn and each driver thought the other responsible. As a result, several adverse comments were made and Bill Rucker got in the first punch, which in most cases determines the outcome.

An attempt was made to ban each driver for a year, but after several committee meetings, both drivers were reprimanded and the affair ended. Neither driver took long term offense and general tranquility resumed.

It was generally known that Harry had been a black belt Kurate athlete. I asked him "Harry, a black belt is supposed to be aware. You called in question Reicher's character, what did you expect him to do?!!" He replied with old prize fight credo—"I forgot to duck!"

The Fuller Factor

Lon Stevens purchased a thirteen foot runabout in 1955. He had a good country PR and put himself mid-pack in the races on the West Coast.

Someone told him to send the rotary valve to Henry Fuller and have it rebuilt. Fuller had the reputation of making a valve so efficient that you could spin it and come back ten minutes later, and it would still be spinning!

Long received the rotary shortly before the 1956 APBA Alky Nationals at Long Beach Marine Stadium. The Stadium is the famous single buoy turn venue that is the curse of drivers since it was constructed for the rowing events of the 1932 Olympics.

1954 Long Beach Marine Stadium

A group of C service Alky runabouts approach the start of a heat. The three boats on the left are "banana" style. C-121 is homemade.

C-290 driven by Henry Wagner, Fresno, was the first flat deck runabout built. It was called the "box". Reign of the flat deck was from 1954 to 1974, a generation. Not bad for a design to be competitive that long in a sport where change in constant. Of course, as time went on, the design went through some change.

The boat was made to look better and change such as fin placement and a rail was introduced in 1965 to lift boat more easily by a pit crew as the motor is cranked.

On Wednesday Stevens said that the boat had an excessive bow movement and asked us to check the bottom. Sure enough, the bottom had a serious bump. We took the boat to Culver City (Thirty-five miles), where a power sander was used to correct the problem.

This was the era prior to polyester or Epoxy resin so that bottom was sealed with lacquer. Wax paper was put on the trailer bolsters and off he went. He was advised to put on several more coats of lacquer before the boat hit the water.

Long and his crew put the boat in their motel room and added more lacquer that night.

The race was expected to be won by one of the legends of PR racing—Bill Tenney, Rocky Stone, Stan Leavendusky, Art Pierre, Bud Wiget, Homor Kincaid, Bill Schuyler, Buzz Miller, Herb Rimlinger, or several others. But Lon Stevens got great starts and finished the two heats first and second, for an overall first place and the Championship in C racing runabout—a remarkable achievement by a newcomer to the sport.

Later, Lon said, "The Filler rotary helped me about one and a half or two miles per hour. Fuller also told me where to set the spark time and that did it!"

******

Terry Witham - He started his boat racing when he became old enough to drive a JV runabout. His father, Louis, and Harry Brinkman built the boat and motor for terry.

They won a National Championship and set a Kilo record. But, they were just getting started. Over the next few years, Terry entered the larger horsepower classes and all with great success.

The photo is of Terry winning the A modified runabout APBA Championship in 1986. He won several more in that class, then moved into C modified runabout. He got hold of Gary Miller's outfit and added 5 more championships to that already legendary rig.

1946 Long Beach

C-84 Bert Ball, Glendale, CA, C-12 Bud Wiget, Pasadena, CA, C-18 Pat Freeman, Ventura, CA

Bert Ball, teamster, was the person who said several years later, "Look it's a Cab Over!" When the first of that design appeared. He had started driving an Evinrude Speedi-twin C Service motor in 1937. Note that in 1946 the motors still used the factory muffler and the transom height was 17".

Bud Wiget had started racing prior to WWII and had just graduated from Caltech and was about to seriously begin a boat racing career.

Pat Freeman was another veteran boat driver. He had started in the early '30's. At one time Pat had held the C Service competition record and was always a front-runner.

Ball and Freeman did their own motor work. Wiget usually had Ernie Millot do most of his important motor work. Bert Ball was also well renowned for his ability to keep his CORD auto in running condition.

Wiget is driving a Rockholt runabout, the other's have DeSilva.

The 4/60 Strikes Again!

George Peake was a very good foundry man. Pep Hubbell was lucky to have found such a good source for all the metal castings an outboard motor manufacturer needed. Generally, when George had a Hubbell pattern with a flow or problem he corrected it.

After a few years Peake became interested enough in Hubbell's sport to try driving a race boat. Pep provided a hydro for an initial exposure and George shortly thereafter decided to buy an F hydro outfit. The 4-60 motor and hydro is no tame beast, but he was a big, tough man and felt that he could cope.

All this took place in the early '50's. Joe swift was making a very successful line of hydros at his plant in Mt. Dora, Florida, George, impressed with all this success, bought the largest Swift available— the eleven footer, which was designed and built for the large Stock racing motor, the Mercury KG9.

George was told that the boat was not constructed for the weight and torque of a 4-60, that it probably would present some problems.

Nonetheless, at a Long Beach Marine Stadium regatta in 1954, George put the brand new boat in the water. In the early morning testing he ran around the course several times, then headed out to the channel entrance, out of sight.

Some time later George appeared in the pits, soaking wet and no boat. When asked what happened, he replied, "I was going along okay when all of a sudden I found myself in the water. I don't know what happened, but the boat is a mess—the patrol boat is bringing it back now."

The boat had no transom and no motor. It was evident that the transom had fractured and the motor had dragged George out of the boat when the steering wheel and cable had followed the motor.

George was very lucky. He came out of the accident with only hurt feelings. The motor was found several days later, but the boat was a total loss.

1984 Livermore Dam, California

Buzz Miller, Galt, California, encounters some rough water. His 44 CID modified Mercury pushes the runabout at a speed of about 75 mph.

In 1946, Miller achieved his 15 minutes of fame. The USA National Championships for Alky runabouts were to be held at Lake Mead (boulder Dam) Nevada. The weather turned nasty and the race was cancelled- rescheduled to Salton Sea, a few days later. A few drivers went home. The race group departed for the Sea where again the water forced a cancellation. The race was then postponed to the next weekend at Long Beach marine Stadium, where the weather had never been an adverse factor. A few more drivers went home.

Two weeks after the first attempt, a race was held at Marine Stadium. It is true that some competitors were missing, but among those who stick it out was Buzz Miller, who won both heats of C runabout with his PR and a National Championship.

Left- William Fales out of that Coterie, which emerged out of Long Island, NY after WWII.

And what a group it was! With the possible exception of Southern California that area produced a group of outboard racing drivers, entrepreneurs and officials without equal.

Bill's forte was the big motors. He started with the Evinrude 460 and at one time or another ran everything from a C Crescent to a 6 cylinder Mercury. He may have had a hydro or two, but his

affection was given to the runabout.

Over the years, he was several times a national champion, chairman of the Alky APBA commission, local referee and often a motor inspector.

His original occupation was chemical engineer and spend the latter part of his life making exotic racing fuels and lubricants for the boat and auto racing clans.

Right- It is hard to imagine anyone dominating a class as Harry Brinkman, Indiana did. APBA and NOA C modified runabout in the '70's and '80's.

Harry was on medical sick leave from his occupation – airplane tower operator, when President Reagan fired the striking operators and replaced them with Army personnel. Harry escaped with a job and a pension.

His expertise will the Mercury 30H was legendary. He could get more out of the motor than anyone. In fact, he wrote a book on how to turn and modify a Mercury that is considered a bible today.

Harry won a number of NOA and APBA National Championships and several Kilo and competition records. Terry Witham won a half-dozen with a C runabout and Gary Miller, Indiana did the same with his equipment. And, it seems likely that George Luce will do the same with Gary's old motor.

Harry was a master at driving a chine-turn runabout. He would put his chest on the left cowl and spin around a buoy so tight paint would scrape off the boat.

Photo-Whipple

The Kingsberg Riddle.

O.S Christener of Quincy, began making an impact on boat racing during middle '50's.

We had sold a small racing runabout to a boat and motor company in St. Louis, for use with what they said would be a SR Johnson. Through a process unknown, Quincy Welding obtained the boat for their modified Mercury motors.

We started to hear of remarkable results from this combination. One member of the Quincy driving team was Fred Goehl, who had gone through a kilo trap at over sixty miles per hour in one of our runabouts. Alren Crouch and David Christner were also prominent.

We got a call from O.F. requesting a new boat similar to the one they had obtained in St. Louis. We questioned the request because the boat had not been designed for the Mercury motor. Mr. Christner said the boat was very good for the Mercury and the speed they were getting with that combination. They wanted another just the same.

During the next twenty years we had a very successful association with Quincy Welding. Because Quincy had many drivers, we often sold them a number of boats each year.

It was almost impossible to keep the Quincy team out of a Championship class, because they would throw driver after driver at a qualification heat till they were fully engaged.

Chris would preach to his drivers, "I don't care how fast we're going—we set up to win boat races, and the race doesn't necessarily go to the swift, it goes to the best boat around the course."

This small, limited resource company more than just kept pace with foreign and domestic competitors. We doubt that Quincy effort was helped technically by the Mercury Outboard Corporation. Christener's business ambition was to obtain a good customer base, then have that base sustain him through parts and improved motor technology. "If I have X numbers and can get them to spend XX with me each year, I'll do ok," he remark.

It was an interesting contest. At various times Quincy battled with Konig, OMC, Yamato and Anzani. No brand dominated for long. Some, like the Anzani, were very successful in classes A and B for a number of years while Bill Tenney was active and interested.

The main contest seemed to be between Konig and Quincy, especially in the larger class. For many years the screech of Quincy open exhaust pipes was a source of public wonder. It has long been felt that the beast of the Merc mega-phone exhaust contributed to a general loss of hearing within the racing fraternity. The introduction of Konig's closed expansion chamber pipe system, in the '60's, was a welcome relief.

Quincy Welding had the Indian sign on big Mercury's. The 44 CID Merc with a Quincy full house makeup was a wondrous sight indeed.

Once, Fred Hauenstein, Sr. and Ed Karakawa decided to have Quincy modify a motor for them. They would then so work on a couple of their own power heads. The Quincy motor proved to be a wonder. Fred was a good mechanic and Ed a farmer with all-round capability—so the modification copy would be no problem, right? They spent all of one winter on several power heads. When spring arrived they were ready. Except—"We're several miles short. Let's go back and check everything. Maybe we made some mistakes. Ok, Let's try again. Still short!"

The two could never make their own motor go as well as the original Quincy.

This is a head scratcher. It's said that there's no secret to making a motor go—if everything is square and set up right, it has to go. Right, but not exactly. Not really.

Many experts have tried to duplicate a Tom Newton-built Evinrude C Service motor. None that we know of have ever succeeded. Walk Blankenstein always seemed to get more out of a motor than other motor specialists. Henry Fuller could make a PR rotary valve better than his competition. Alan Smith could make a propeller go faster than other specialists.

It has always been a source of wonder as to why some are able to obtain a better result. Most agree that after a good bit of time spend on an endeavor one will develop a feel for the task. Apparently it took Tom Edison ninety-plus experiments before he arrived at a working light bulb. Experimentation, trial and error, study, and testing all contribute—but with a hefty dose of talent!

1976 700cc World Championship

Site for this great regatta was Firebird Lake, Pheonix, Arizona.

There were several foreign teams on had – the Japanese with their Yamato motors; and the German team powered by Konig.

Hans Kraage, West Berlin, flew to Atlanta where he joined with the Charly's Angel team headed by Charles Westbrook, Marietta, They then trailed to Arizona with a trailer filled with boats and motors.

Kraage was a famous European outboard racing champion. He drove only Konig racing motors and any good competition boat – all hydroplanes and especially the lay-down call over – European style.

The Americans were only able to provide token competition to their high flying German. Hans won in a convincing manner over 2nd place Bill Rucker, Oakland, who drove a 6 cylinder Mercury on a conventional 3 pt. hydro.

Kraage subsequently returned many times to the US. His English improved and his open personality made many friends.

With hat – David Westbrook
Hans Kraage

Not so Typical

You would think that over a span of many years we would have had many persons walk into the shop and say, "I want to get involved in boat racing, can you help me?" Not so.

I can only remember one time like that.

A very young couple walked into the Culver City shop one day and made the above request. The teenager was Walter Huhn, then going to high school, and the girl was his bride to be, Betty.

They were a splendid couple: he strong, tall and very bright. Betty was a knockout— blond and a perfect compliment.

Of course we did everything necessary to get Walter involved. Probably because he had the interest, drive and intent, he became what could be characterized as a premier boat racer in the stock division.

Walter became the manager of a mid-sized company serving the aircraft and allied industries located in the East LA area. They moved to West Covina to be closer to the company, so Bill and I did not see the as frequently, but the relationship continued throughout his driving career which lasted into the seventies.

Sometime in the '60's, Walter decided to attend the Alky Nationals in Midland Michigan, way up the Michigan peninsula. He had a Mercury 44 CID and a D Runabout to compete with the Konig and Quincy Merc's. Walt knew he was outclassed by some of the exotic reg's, but "you can't win 'em all, can you?" He was there for the fun of it—perhaps the experience of a lifetime.

The stock Nationals were to be held the next weekend at Guntersville, Alabama. Walter and Betty drove down for that. Now the stock division was Walter's forte; he was a competitor. Should he be able to go fast as he had been going in California, why, he should have a chance.

Conditions at Guntersville were normal for the South at the time of year: hot and humid. California would have been very dry and mild. The carburation and propeller situations were different. Walt found that he was several mph short of what he had obtained in CA. Even after several days of testing he could not find the solution.

He had no trouble qualifying for the final D runabout. First heat, he got a fair start, got into the turn 4th and worked himself into 3rd. Second heat he was able to drive himself into the same position for an overall 3rd place. Not bad for an outfit that was not performing at top efficiency.

Above- 1976 Lodi California

A customer who has a Mercury six cylinder motor and wants a good hydro is a customer who presents problems.

There is probably no way to design a really good race boat for that motor. It is top heavy, has a ton of torque and the quicksilver lower unit will win no prizes. The best solution would be a Tunnel, but that design is outlawed in Pro racing.

A 15' three-point hydro was built for Casey Parsons. The boat was reasonably successful and Casey drove the boat with confidence. He was more successful with his KR/Mercury combo- which at one time held a APBA F runabout competition record at 96+mph.

Below- 1976 Tom Gouldstone

Tom, Napa, drives a Yamato 80 on his C stock runabout.

He had just resumed boat racing after a 15 year interval. Born and raised in the Los Angeles area, Tom and his father Jack and started outboard racing when the APBA stock division began in 1947.

The model 80 arrived in the US about 1965, sold for about $300 and pushed a runabout 60 mph.

Catch Me If You Can

Peter Kugener, an Australian, appeared on the Southern California racing scene in the mid-'60's.

He'd married a local girl and opened a successful boat repair and painting operation in the San Fernando Valley.

We used him for some of our boat painting since his work was really good. He finished the hydro we built for Mr. McCulloch, head of his corporation. McColluch had raced on outboard during his college days, so folks in his organization thought a birthday present of a new hydro mated to a 590 motor would be a present surprise. Everyone thought the boat was beautiful. Because the boat was to be a presentation and an object of admiration, no thought was given to weight.

Pete was not a young man. He had piloted a Mosquito fighter plane during World War Two—till a belly landing due to faulty landing gear had washed him out.

He put together an Alky B hydro outfit and became a respectable competitor. Pete may not have been a front runner, but he was having fun.

After a divorce, there may have been some rancor because his wife notified the U.S. immigration that Pete was not a citizen. He had thought that marriage to an American would take care of his legal status and had done nothing to be naturalized. He dodged authorities for about a year, then was put on a plane for Canada.

I got a call from his several months later. He was still dodging immigration—this time, the Mounted Police! He had come to the US in order to experience how we did things. He liked the US and decided to stay a while. He probably never intended to become a US citizen and was not entirely unhappy to be invited to leave. Canada was not his preference and it was generally thought that he eventually ended back in Australia.

Pete was a free spirit, fill of fun, with a streak of deviltry. He probably delighted in the tweak of authority.

After all, life didn't have much beyond spending time in the cockpit of a mosquito—hearing the grown of the plywood and seeing the wings flap somewhat like a bird. No worries—plywood will float, and so what that I'm several hundred miles over the ocean!

1966 Southern Cross Marine

Peter Kugener, Austrailia, Standing left, in front of the McCulloch Corp. Showboat built for the display of their 590, 3 cylinder motor.

Kugener was an expert painter and detail man so we let him do a fine finish one the exhibition boat. It traveled throughout the US during the boat show exhibition season.

The boat was an 18' twin engine, two cockpit 3 point hydro design to simulate a competition race boat.

Peter Kugener was divorced by an American wife and was deported back to Australia shortly after this photo.

Pure Logic

Let's deal in a little fantasy and some logic.

Plato and Socrates are having a seminar. Socrates says, "Let us talk about logic — the human condition is based on logic and fact. What is logic? Simply put it is the way of correct thought. You have two sticks: fact. You add two more sticks and you have four sticks: fact. That is simple logic."

Here is another example. This one is a true story that takes place sometimes in the early '50's; once upon a time in the West.

During the early years of Stock racing category there were many Marathons—especially popular were those held on the Colorado River around Needles, CA. Beginning in the late '40's, Needles was the starting line for the annual Marathon from Needles to Topock and back: about seventy-five miles.

There is nothing to commend Needles. Except for wintertime, the desert is noted for high daytime temperatures. Spring and summer days of one hundred degrees are the norm. The town itself is only a brief stop on what is now Interstate Highway 10. But, at the time of this episode it was a gas station or two on Route 66.

Both sides of the river, from fifty to one hundred miles, is pure desert, inhabited by snakes, lizards, and small rodent. Although most desert areas cool off considerably during the night, around Needles it is not uncommon to have a midnight temperature into the '90's. This is probably due to the humidity coming from the river.

At this time the 36 CID runabout class was not popular nation-wide, but it did have a considerable following in California. There were probably fifteen or twenty 36's registered in the area. Dan Swartzenbach was the leader of this group and had worked hard to build up the class. He operated a small boat shop in the LA area and his store was headquarters for the group.

Because of their slow speed the 26 class started first, with AU runabout second.

Ron Hill, a very young man, had started boat racing in the A class. Sometime after the race began, Ron pulled up on Dan's 36 and noticed a beer can flying out. A short time later another came floating by.

All the way to Topock and back to Needles there were beer cans floating on the water. Ron told his father, Russ, who was a race referee, "Pop, I saw Swartzenbach and some other of those 36 drivers ditching empty beer cans all over the river!"

Russ Hill stomped over to Dan Swartzenback in the pit area and announced, "I'm going to throw you out—you were drinking!"

Dan replied, "Well yeah, but there is nothing in the rule book that says I can't drink while driving the boat. How can you throw me out?"

Russ, nonplussed and no stranger to a beer can, looked at Dan for a moment, shrugged, smiled and walked away.

Plato can pause for a moment and say, "That is an example of pure logic." Socrates replies, "Two and two make four."

[Note: The APBA changed the alcohol rule because of this incident: "No contestant shall participate in a race, nor she any official serve in an official capacity after having consumed alcohol or controlled substances or while intoxicated. The phrase 'after having consumed...or intoxicated' shall mean from midnight before the of the race and until the driver has been cleared through inspection."]

Handling the Bow

Russ Hill was a tall, fun-loving house painter with a wife, two sons, and a home in Bellflower, California.

He became involved in boat racing, and we first met Russ in 1946 at a Long Beach marine Stadium regatta. Russ had acquired a PR-65 and ordered a new runabout. He named the boat "FOREVER AMBER" and painted it a vivid purple. The name originated via a notorious novel by Kathleen Windsor which had dominated post-war seller lists.

Outboard racing in Southern California began a solid growth after WWII. There were a few pre-war motors available and Pep Hubbell had arrived in Rosemead and had begun to make replacement parts and even complete motors. Ex-Navy pumper units could be had very cheaply and be converted to a racing motor.

Despite intense pressure the OMC factory decided not to resume manufacture of racing motors. Hubbel promised to provide parts and motors to keep outboard racing alive.

The speed of a class C runabout at that time was in the area of 48-53 mph. Out runabout was typical. Because speeds were moderate, a runabout design at that time would today be called dynamic. On the other hand, they were not overly hard to control. Performance (as always) depended upon setup and driver skill.

It could be said that Russ, as a novice driver, tended to be a loose cannon. Long Beach Marine Stadium was the venue for three or four races per year—sponsored by various organizations, clubs or newspapers. The Stadium was certainly a difficult race course for most drivers: a long, narrow body of brackish water, sand on both sides and rocks on shore, coming out of the single buoy first turn.

Some ten years later in 1956, and APBA Alky Nationals Championship was held at the stadium. The Eastern drivers took one look at the site—and refused to participate. After much agitation, they ended up racing, but most of them did not do well. Wind was never a problem, so the water smooth, except for that churned up by the boats themselves. Most flips at the stadium were roll-overs.

Therefore there was no recognized altitude record for a back flip at Long Beach. It has long been said that Russ Hill holds the record for that performance in 1956. He must have had a splendid view of Catalina Island, twenty miles off the coast. All in all a great effort!

Sometime after his altitude attempt, Russ was involved in an episode which required us to re-design a piece of boat hardware. My father had admired the hood ornaments of several autos and had carved a rather unique wood pattern for a runabout bow handle—handsome in form, with a slightly pointed rear. No point in front, so no hazard—right? Wrong?

At Lake Elsinore regatta, Russ came into the puts after a test run. Either the throttle stuck or he forgot to release the automatic hand throttle, because the boat hit the beach and headed for down-town. He polished his prop and lower unit nicely in the soft sand, cleared any barnacles off the boat bottom and propelled himself over the deck in fine horizontal style. The only obstacle between himself and a line of cars was our bow handle. Hill, quick and agile as he was, put out his hand and encountered the bow handle. We changed our bow handle and Russ Hill only temporarily became one-handed.

77T Miss Laurie

It is remarkable for a race boat – any race boat, to have a career of over 20 years,

Bruce Nicholson, Texas, purchased the third KR built in 1974. Twenty years later, he was driving the same boat and as successfully as in the early years. The motors, C, D & F became obsolete; but the 77T soldiered on.

77T was eventually retired sometime in the '90's, to the ceiling of a Florida restaurant.

KR

We have often been asked how the name KR came about and what it means. This name was given to a new boat introduced in 1974.

The Alky division had originally established racing runabout rules at Salton Sea in 1947. George Mishey had built a runabout for a Texas driver who attended the California race. This boat created a fire-storm. It had a spoon bow, very low sides, with extreme tumble home. It was indeed a handsome boat, but far adrift of accepted runabout standards. Mishey was essentially a builder of hydros—the boat seemed fine to him.

1947 Salton Sea

This is the '47 Mishey built boat that created the modern Alky runabout measurement rules that have governed the division ever since.

The runabout created an adverse reaction that demanded standards that would stabilize the sport.

A drivers meeting held with the racing commission resulted in a rejection of the Mishey boat and establishment of a new runabout measurement rules. There really had been no prior definite standard, except for weight and length. All the various boat brands were examined and a consensus was established.

We completed testing the first KR in late 1973 and started selling them in 1974.

Homer Kincaid was chairman of the APBA Alky Commission at that time. We had a discussed change with Homer over a period of time.

He also felt that it was time for change and that the runabout could and should be improved in performance. Homer was not a reactionary. His attitude was in opposition to those who claim, "I'm all for safety." But then run in the opposite direction when faced with action. He said, "Let's go with some change. If you can design a better boat, I'm all for it."

We were looking for stability at the ever increasing speeds produced by the modern outboard motors. The only restriction placed on motors was applied to bore and stroke. This had resulted, over the years, in speeds that were not compatible with boat designs.

We realized that boat racing is no different than any other activity—folks are reluctant to accept change. Anything beyond the present comfort zone is to be avoided.

Ultimately, we came up with something which would allow change, but not so much that it would cause heartburn.

We wanted stability at speeds over 85 mph. Beneath that speed a runabout can be designed to perform with reasonable stability and turning capability. Above such speed, the design does present problems. This can be said of all small boats, hydro or runabout. At extreme high speed one does not have a boat— the object is then an airplane.

Water is dense, whereas air is much less so. An object will go much faster in air than through water. This is elementary. We had placed the fin as much as 12" off center, to no advantage. On the contrary, an offset fin gave us real problems. At 6" offset the boat would broach; at 12" the boat would angle to the left with real drag.

We sttled for a small center fin, placed far enough back to the transom to give reliable effect, whatever that happened to be. Because a back-flip has never been acceptable, we made the planning surface relatively long—which contributed to a turn spin. This was a problem until we began using deck down pressure instead of the bottom. Some years later the chine fin placement solved a good many problems for a racing runabout.

As this is written, not many runabouts in the Alky division are the DeSilva brand, but you can be sure that their bottom will be that of the KR. Don't believe that? Look and compare yourself!

Were it not penalized for weight and size restrictions, the runabout would be comparable in performance with the hydroplane. At speed, the runabout has no design impediment—the monoplane has no inherent resistance.

The hydro, in contrast, has the forward sponson (or step) which forces or maintains a trim angle— which produces resistance (drag). Successful record speed hyrdroplanes have slight or almost no forward sponsons—for good reason. The kilo boat should be more airplane rather than boat.

We had been building the flat deck runabout since 1954. Prior to that, our original design was the Banana boat. During the '60's we noticed that the Indy and Grand Prix racing vehicles were using a new form of streamlining. Instead of emphasizing frontal streamlined airflow, they gave attention to down force. And, as Alky race boats were doing the ton, we felt that something would be done about boat down force. The runabout deck seemed to be the area that would afford such capability.

We placed half an in cream cone structure on a 13' runabout. Testing indicated that the boat had less tendency for bow lift and the driver was better able to remove himself from air flow. This was better performance and a more efficient boat. We experimented a bit with cowl length and depth, and determined that beyond a certain amount the result was not measurable. At the same time, we changed from the ship fin to one on the transom.

Boats were being lifted out of the water by the put crew in order to reduce propeller drag while trying to start a reluctant motor. So, we placed a lifting rail on the outside of each chine. This proved to be a definite improvement, and it now standard on most high speed runabouts.

That Homer Kincaid is an icon of boat racing is without question. Not everyone liked him, though he was respected and admired for his capability and talent. He probably was too much of a winner to be universally accepted.

Sometime, someone will write a biography of Homer Kincaid, for there is no one in outboard alky racing who was his master. For now, though, it is logical and right that Homer Kincaid take credit for the Kr: Kincaid's Responsibility. He fathered the design, despite knowing that he would be criticized for doing so.

-1979

A man of many talents, William Fales, Long island and New Jersey was severely bitten by the boat racing bug. He loved the big powerful Alky motors. For many years, mid-century, he was the man to beat in the two man F runabout.

He served as region APBA chairman and was several times leader of the APBA Alky Division. He with sons Rick and Steve, Attended boat races all over the USA. Bill, at one time or another, raced a Crescent, Quincy cross-flow and looper, Konig and 4:60's, PR-65 and Evinrude C Service- whatever was likely to be competitive.

Bill was not a reactionary, he enthusiastically accepted boat and motor innovation, yet acknowledged that it was not in everyone's interest to accept speed for the sake of speed.

He ended his boat racing career as a manufacturer of potent, high tech racing fuel products.

This was an interesting project. Everything was new and untried. The motor was a John Toprahanian project, a Kowasaki motorcycle powerhead mated to a Mercury tower housing and Konig lower unit.

The hydro was special, designed for the power plant. Note the hand throttle—only 6 were made.

Performance was never determined. The motor never ran consistently enough to arrive at a conclusion. John T. became interest in other projects, the motor was set aside and its potential was never fully explored.

Photo-Loomis

Photo- Ted May – driver, Ted May – Deck Rider (not related)

George May was John Toprahanian's driver of choice. Motor is the famous Yama-rudie-which was highly competitive through the '60's and into the early '70's when thereafter the big Konig and Quincy motors began to dominate.

The flat deck runabout design reigned from 1954 till 1974; when the KR took over.

Photo-Delackner

1975 Winona Minnesota

Activity in the puts after a heat of Alky (pro) class C (500 CID) runabout. Dick Hoppenrath, Minnesota, is shown working Jerry Simison's Konig motor. James Aderholt, Godsden, Alabama (54 t-shirt) is an interested observer. On his left is Jerry Simison, receiving a cup of water from an associate. In the water, wearing a lifejacket and holding his boat is Charles Bailey, Houston, Texas.

Jerry Simison, a very young man. He became an Alky outboard racing legend, through many years of successful campaigning. His standard of accomplishment is outstanding. His activity was largely restricted to the runabout which he felt most compatible to his style of driving.

The race course at Winona is within a city park next to the famous Rock Dome in the background.

1975 Winona Minnesota

Fred Havenstein, Jr (left), Fred, Sr., and Bruce Nicholson are all smiles. Well, they should- Fast Fred has just placed third at the APBA Alky National Championships with his brand new Kr runabout and Bruce Nicholson has won the coveted first place also with a new KR.

Not in the photo-Charles Baily, Houston, also in a newly introduced KR got the second place and set a new competition record in one heat. They were all powered by 40 CID German Konig class D motor.

The Sled

Tom Roath was a large marine dealer in Denver. He had been involved with Outboard boat racing for many years despite a location where such activity was minimal. He had driven a competitive PR on a runabout and hydro. We became acquainted at a National Championship and had invited him to race in California. We had not heard from him for a while when we received a call in 1966. He said, "I can get hold of several new Evinrude 4-cylinder motors, and I'd like to have you build me a tunnel for the upcoming Havasu Two Day Marathon."

The deal was made and we began work on a twin engine eighteen foot tunnel boat that we called the sled. The previous year I had been to the Paris Six Hour Marathon on the Seine River. You've never seen rough water till you watch a race on the Seine. The river in downtown Paris has vertical banks from eight to fourteen feet, made of stone and concrete—bridges cross the river every quarter mile. With any sustained disturbance, the water will bounce off these banks with waves that can be horrendous.

We knew that Molinari, the Italian boat builder, would have boats at Havasu and would know how to design a good competitive boat. There would be boats from every builder in the US and other areas of the world. The competition would be as good as it can get.

We knew that Roath's effort would be first class—this would be a great chance to compete! We were not totally inexperienced with tunnel design, having built a few such boats and becoming familiar with most of the problems. We put a considerable amount of time and energy into the boat.

We met with Roath's team at Havasu City a few days before the event and helped with the rig setup. Testing indicated that the sled had a reasonable speed, and handling seemed good. Still, we did not know competition capabilities and so didn't feel confident.

Referr George May had designed an unusual way to keep score over the two day affair. Each team had to provide one person as a representative. As the race progressed, the member would be placed on the grid to indicate the boat position. We have that job to my son Norman. He later said, "I was sitting there, a fifteen year old kid, among a large group of knowledgeable boat people looking at me, probably wondering who and what I was doing there. As they moved me to the head of the group, I'm sure they had some questions!"

As the race progressed on the first day, Roath and his co-driver steadily moved into the lead, among the eighty plus outfits. Among the competitors were single engines, twin and triple engines, tunnels, runabouts, hydros and Switzer Wings.

The race course was about two and a half miles long, with dog legs, right hand turns, left turn, long and short stretches. Some turns were tight and some were sweeping. All in all, a challenge for both man and equipment.

150

Tom was not the fastest, but he had several advantages. The sled could motor through rough water and his punch in and out of the turns was very good. Soon after getting the lead, Tom came into the puts for fuel. Bill and I helped physically to pour gas using five gallon pails. This was inefficient and time consuming, but what could be done on a limited budget. Jack Leek, manager of the OMC factory team, called from across the lagoon and said, "You're welcome to put over here where we can supply fuel with our pressure hose." Subsequently, with that help, Tom was able to hold and help his lead for the remainder of the first day. To be the race leader at the halfway point was a great morale boost. The OMC factory team offered all support—they could see that his independent team could very well win the event.

Tom led through the first hour and a half of the second day. Then, his battery failed. This delay into the puts and prolonged battery replacement resulted in an overall fourth place race finish. But for the mechanical problem, Roath would have won a major US event. It is one thing to do well in an important race, but to do so again world competition was a source of satisfaction.

Note: in 1993 Tom Roath died as a result of a B Alky hydro turnover while testing at Lake Blackshear in South Georgia, with Melvin Cooper and son. Tom was seventy-two years old.

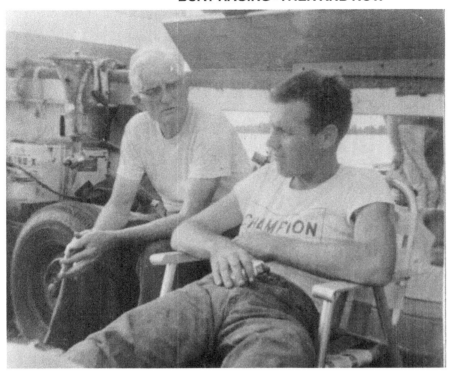

1963 Alexandria LA

Willie A Cooper and son Melvin relax between events at the NOA National Championship regatta.

The competition at Alex was always fierce. The site was famous for its fast water and pit conditions—a very good race boat venue in a central location for drivers from each coast.

Carl Rylee, the race promoter, did his best to make the race a must-do event.

Fort Buhlow Lake is on the Red river between Alexandria and Pineville. The lake is about a mile long and ¼ mile wide. The lake gets its name from a bluff over the river called Fort Buhlow—where a battle for the city of Alexandria was fought during the Civil War. On one bank of the lake is an airstrip, used by small aircraft.

1966 Paris France

These three photos indicate the chaotic water conditions on the Seine River during the six hour endurance.

The race had been an annual event through the 1970 when it was cancelled after a number of casualties.

It was clear that the race conditions at the event could not be controlled and the accident rate could not be accepted by either the participants or the public.

1975 San Diego

George May, left and John Toprahanian stand next to trophies won during the successful 1975 racing season.

Their equipment is the famous Yamarudi motor design and put together by John and their 14' flat deck F runabout.

John designed the motor a few years previous to the photo. The components were Yamaha cylinders attached to a 4:60 Evinrude crankcase. John also had a gear case where different gear ratios could be changed relatively easily.

During the '30's, John had raced a 10' hydro – SR Johnson powered. He worked at the San Diego Naval shipyard, retired after WWII and then devoted his life to work and design racing motors for boats and 4:60 midget race cars.

John chose George May as his driver after doctors told him that driving race boats was too strenuous for his heart condition.

George switched from his B stock runabout to the F effortlessly and one can see that the result of their teamwork was excellent.

I Want a Free Boat!

Prior to the move to Georgia, we had sold a few boats to drivers in New England. Bill Fales of New York City had been a longtime customer, as were a few drivers from Long Island such as Peter Voss, Doug Bindrim, Bob Houghkirk, Pete Hellsten, and others.

But shortly after the shop was setup in Dallas, Georgia, we received an influx of Modified Division customers from that area. We had never been big with the Modified Division although Harry Brinkman and Lou Witham and his son Terry had been very successful for a number of years. Our problem, most likely, was the Modified drivers trying to use Alky boats with Modified motors. We had, for many years, tried to explain that a boat successful in one division would not necessarily be good in another. In the very early years of boat racing, the use of one boat for several divisions may have been possible because the disparity in speed was not marked. But, as the speed deferential between the various drivers was so wide, it was a necessary to employ a different design.

The first DeSilva boat Quincy welding used was a second hand boat we had originally sold to a customer in St. Louis. O.F. Christner called us and wanted another just like it. I asked what kind of motor he'd use, and in which division. He said a Merc and the Alky division. This boat was special: the customer had an Sr Johnson he wanted to use on the boat. It was a big longer and heavier with a longer cockpit than what we would have built for a stock or mod boat. The Alky division had created new classes for a runabout: A and B. Mr. Christner wanted to campaign his Mercury motor in these new divisions. I told Chris that I would like to build him a boat more suited to the Alky division. He said, "No, the boat we have is just what we need, but I have more than one driver and we several more boats just like this."

For whatever reasons, the Modifieds took in the New England during the early '80's. We sold 8-10 boats over a short period of time and I thought the area would really bloom.

One day we got a call from a fellow who said he was Don Fryklund, a building contractor in West Gloucester, Massachusetts, and needed a new boat, not just any boat—it had to be special. "I want a boat that talks to me. It has to be a high flyer, I want it to be dynamic and loose. I have a Ron Hill boat built by Lee Morehouse. It is OK, but a bit too heavy with a poor turning hull. Can you help me?"

Now, we have had a good many unusual requests but that was the first time anyone had ever asked for a dynamic, loose riding boat! Talk about modified! Usually the request for just the opposite: most drivers want a docile, conservative approach—one with which they feel comfortable. Still, nothing pleases a race boat builder more than to have a customer request a dynamic boat. All race boats are dynamic—it's a question of degree. The problem and question is, with how much dynamism can one cope?

During that era, in the mid '80's, one could not sell a Mod or Stock boat unless it was a chine turner. We had worked on that design for some time and felt that we had a good competitive boat. At the 1983 APBA Stock Nationals Dave Bryan had

5H was one of a series built in the early 1980's. At that time it was difficult to sell a runabout if it was not a chine-turn design.

Harry Brinkman had insisted in 1978 that the chine-turn design was the way to go. OK, we built several models, the last which could be said was a real prop-out-of-the-water chine turner. It made Brinkman happy and we sold a good number in the Midwest and New England through the '80's.

Gary Miller, Indiana, obtained one of these boats – the 5H. It together with a Brinkman built Mercury 30H C Modified motor, won 5 National Championships.

The boat was sold to Terry Witham, a Brinkman clan member and the young man won another huge number of championships.

A number of Yomato motors tried for years but were never able to beat the 5H, although other Mercury motors gave up the contest.

The day of the chine turn race boat is over, but they had a good run and everyone had fun. The chine fin, flat turn boat is a superior design.

won a C Stock Runabout using one of the chine turn boats. We were not entirely sold on the design—we felt the design scrubbed too much speed going through the turns. How much push is obtained with the propeller out of the water? However, the look is spectacular—it's cool. That may be the reason for the design's poularity. So we gave Don a chine turner, super light, and we "freed" the boat as much as thought any responcible driver could handle. Handle it he could and did. Don Fryklund turned out to be a major force in the New England with the new boat.

Don had a brother who drove hydros. The brother bought one of the new 75HP Johnson 3 cylinder motors. He found it almost unmanageable on a hydro and turned it over to Don for possible use on the runabout. The motor was a legal D mod class unit with a tremendous torque and punch. Don phoned and reported that the motor and boat resulted in a package that was almost more than he could handle. He decided it enter it as a legal entry at the APBA Modified Nationals, in Formula E. His competition would be the Mercury 44 CID and perhaps other Evinrude 75's. Although the Evinrude was too heavy for his 13' runabout and the torque was somewhat beyond his control, he decided to participate with what he had.

In the first heat Don got a great start, quickly finding himself in the lead going into the first turn. It was soon evident that there was no competitor who would present a problem, so he was able to win the head with a comfortable margin. Rather than take a change on jumping the gun in the second heat, he crossed the line well behind the clock. Don came out of the first turn behind several boats but was able to place himself in first comfortably, and won the heat and the championship.

He later told us that he was not comfortable driving the big Evinrude motor and decided not to further campaign in Formula E. Fryklund's evaluation of the Evrinrude 75 turned out to be on the mark. The motor never achieved any popularity. It only found a home in the OPC category, where it has powered tunnel class SST60's. The tunnel hull could accommodate the motor, torque and weight.

Don Fryklund became an outstanding competitor. He was fortunate in having a good relation with Robert Goller who's motors were first rate. Throughout the 80's, we often heard of the boat battles between Fryklund, the Fales and George Lace. When Mr. Robert Goller worked on Don's motors, he was the man to beat.

In now seems evident that the 1986 Safe Daisy Modified Nationals was the zenith of that division. The entry list of boats form New England area was remarkable. For many reasons—some known and some unknown—the attrition has been such that at the moment there are not enough entries to make a successful regatta.

Don Fryklund phone recently to say hello and to reminisce of the old days. Proof that boat racing is a disease that never leaves the system, he said, "I'd love to race again, but my body says forget it." I told him he had better come back soon—otherwise I probably would not be around to build him a new boat.

My Way

1995 Westerman Jones

He was a perfectionist. No half measures for Jones – it had to be perfect. When asked why he wanted to make his own PR-65 cylinders he said, "The factory cylinders had a tendency to crack at the base, where the stud entered the barrel. I made a stronger cylinder base with better material." Over the years he sold hundreds of cylinders – which are acknowledged as the best. He thought the Vincent PR cylinders were about as good but felt that his material may be a bit better. He had spent considerable time and treasure with engineers in order to find the formula.

The motors he personally put together were as fine an example of workmanship as can be found in boat racing. They were beautiful. They may have been too pretty, too tight. But when they did run as expected they were awesome.

One year he had Matt D'Agustino drive his equipment at the DePue Alky Nationals. Matt won the first two heats with the class C antique runabout but could not start in the 3rd final heat. The end result was second place. For some reason, the ignition system failed.

Sometimes it took a while for Jones motors to loosen up – especially in the transition from magnets to battery ignition.

Westerman W. Jones was born and raised in Delaware. His father was a successful businessman who wanted his son to get a good education in order to be successful as well. He wanted Wes to attend one of the Ivy League schools.

Westerman, however, wanted a softer climate and less structure, so they motored South toward Florida. But they stopped at Duke University to look around. Duke was a relatively new school then, the campus was beautiful and Wes decided to give it a try.

Later in life he said, "I did not graduate. It was not their fault; I was impatient, and listening to all that theory was okay, but I wanted to put all that stuff to work now, and I didn't want to wait around."

He started a valve business. Valves may not seem to be a great business, but they are universally used item in virtually all manufacturing. And some of Jones's friends were a part of the Dupont family or were associated with the company so he was able to develop a good volume business.

His boat racing career started in 1936-7 with a class F hydro outfit. In 1951 he purchased a PR-65 and Jacoby hydro—and began a love affair with that class. Not happy with the Johnson factory cylinder, he began to manufacture his own.

Both Johnson and Evinrude had decided not to make racing motors or replacement parts after World War Two, though a few individuals, like Jones began to make the parts.

Randolph Hubbell moved to Rosemead, California in 1946 and began to make replacement motors and parts. For many years his replica PR-65, SR and various parts for other motors enable outboard racing to carry on in the US.

Frank Vincent, a pre-war driver began a speed-shop service with some replacement parts. Clyde Wiseman, a journeyman machinist, added a parts service to his boat race driving. His pistons and a C Service lower unit were considered top quality. There was a demand for such equipment, and most suppliers did quite well.

A few individuals worked on a particular item or service. Mel Ezzo made a good Evinrude C Service crankcase—one in which a top bearing could be installed. Marshal Eldredge came up with a nice C

Service lower unit, with your choice of gears, as did Tom Goslee or Arkansas. Hershel Starnes, of North Carolina, made a very good PR lower unit.

Wes Jones did not do anything half-way. It had to be strong—super strong. And he did not like change. When he first ordered a hydro from us, he wanted it to look like a 1935 Jacoby. It's okay to have a modern bottom, but the deck has to low

1956 Long Beach Marine Stadium, What does it take to win the first heat of the APBA National Championship C Hydro, then fall out of your boat in the second.

First, you have to have a set of Wes Jones PR cylinders, a worked rotary valve by Henry Fuller, then a solid tune-up via the Offenhauser dyno and then perhaps a propeller worked by Allen Smith.

Dr. Wayne Ingalls put everything together for son, Tom, who began boat racing as a high school student in Bell, California.

Tom's career as a dentist had just started. He had little time to keep in good physical shape – and found that the exertions at the regatta took so much out of him that he was unable to cope with the tense demands of boat racing – especially at the most demanding of them all – a National Championship.

On Monday after the race, a Kilo record venue was offered, Jack maypole's son, John, went through the timing their PR hydro at a speed of 69+ mph. Tom's Keller speedometer reading prior to the race was 72 mph.

and flat. It took several boats and some arm twisting before he was convinced that we were living another era where some good changes had been made.

His replacement parts were the best. Dr. Wayne Ingalls purchased a set of PR cylinders in 1953. He also sent a rotary valve to Henry Fuller. Ingalls and son Tom put everything on the Meyer/Drake dyno. They tweaked a fiddled until the motor ran very well. The Doctor told us that the Jones set of barrels picked up about 2 mph.

At the 1956 APBA National Championship regatta in Long Beach Marine Stadium, Tom won the first head of C hydro—and but for an unfortunate motor ignition problem, in the pits, which resulted in Tom's physical mishap in the 1st turn of the 2nd heat, he would have won the event, since he was obviously faster than his competition. At the same race Henry Wagner, of Fresno won the C Service hydro class. His hydro was similar in design to the Ingalls boat. Wagner had borrowed Manuel Carnakis's Newton built C Service motor.

1992 Canton Georgia

a

Left to right: Henry Shakeshaft, Westerman Jones, Bill DeSilva

The name Shakeshaft became prominent in the '30's. Elinore was a major "M" hydro driver and Henry drove some of the big outboards with great success.

For many years, and as this is written, a motor using either Westerman Jones or Frank Vincent PR cylinders is considered superior.

Sometime in the 1990's he phoned and asked about going to Florida with him to attend World Championship. He arrived in a 1965 Chevy pickup. No air-conditioning: a bare bones vehicle. He had three or four other vehicles, but the truck had four brand new tires and only 35,000 miles—so no problem. Right?

Wes Jones can be termed one of the "giants" of outboard racing. His after-market products were prominent prior to WWII and are a vital part of equipment used today. His personality and ability can be called genius.

We got down to Florida near Jacksonville, when one of the tires started a serious thump. The tire had a big lump on one sidewall. We drove to the nearest Firestone dealer. Firestone had won an Indy for many, many years so they had to be good. Wes was perturbed, but not concerned— the tire would be replaced and we would be on our way. The Firestone folks looked at the tire, removed it and disappeared for a bit of time. Finally the manager told Wes, "Your tire is over 25 years old and out of warranty."

Wes replied, "The tire is brand new; you can still see the nibs on the side—what does age have to do with the situation?"

Firestone: "We don't guarantee a tire beyond a reasonable amount of time, which is much less than five years, and your tires are over 25 years old. The rubber on the tire will deteriorate. All we can do is give you a discount on four new tires. Your old ones are worthless."

We swallowed hard and bough four new tires—we had no more tire trouble. To purchase a new vehicle plus for additional tires is not something often done, but this sort of thing would not be unusual for Jones.

Having dinner with Wes Jones was not an adventure. It had to be simple; he was a meat and potato man—no Mexican, Chinese, or Indian. "I don't like oregano or garlic—nothing hot. Clam chowder, boiled lobster, fried oyster are good. Hugh puppies and grits are out!"

This was somewhat of a problem at the APBA Depue, Illinois National, because the two best Mexican restaurants east of the Rockies are located at Peru, just south of I-80. They cook California style which differs from Tex-Mex in that the food is not dry.

1956 Mt. Carmel Illinois NOA Alky Nationals

Left to Right: Clyde Wiseman, Bill DeSilva

Clyde began his boat racing in the Cleveland, Ohio area in the '30's. His equipment was first class (as one would expect from a great mechanical talent).

He was one if the few specialist who kept Alky boat alive through his after-market products (especially pistons). Johnson and Evinrude had ceased manufacturing of racing motors after WWII.

2005

When trophies are handed out, the joke is that George Thornhill, Tacoma, Washington, is always there with his hand out.

A consistent winner with bot his PR-65 and C Service motors George appears to drive both hydro and runabout equally well.

When asked how many championships he has won over the years, George says, "I don't know, but I'd like to win one more!" He probably will.

How About the Tiki!

Mark Twain could have done it justice; just as he did with the Mississippi. Of course he would not have had the majesty of the River and its glorious history – But he would have had its cousin – the Illinois River.

Now the Illinois does not have the character, the romance, the sweep of its relative but the Illinois is worthy of some praise. After all, it was the venue of the first organized, scripted, successful Outboard Boat Racing US Championship in the US in 1927 at Peoria.

There are no jumping frogs or gold fields to help bring back the small river towns along the Illinois – the hay-day of the river towns is gone. The economic life along the river is now transported by the railroads and their over the highway cousins – the heavy truck haulers.

The ingenuity of man has no limit. We should hold a wake for the economic life of the small river towns – not a burial. A pleasant place to live, to fish, to boat, to dream.

Early on, accommodation for travelers along the river was usually a hotel or inn. When the automobile arrived, a tourist cabin complex became popular in the US. Things were limited for early travelers to DePue. There was a three story hotel in downtown Peru, 5 miles east and the Tour-rest Motel. That complex is among the river road from Peru to DePue.

The downtown hotel lasted until the '50's when it was converted to an office complex. The Tour-rest Motel is one of the last of the breed. One does not see many operating tourist cabins in the style of the "old west" these days.

For the convenience of beer drinkers, a 55 gallon container is placed at each door. (that is another story – see volume II.) There is a certain charm about the place – especially if one likes turn of the century rustic.

Highway 80 before the interstate system was no big thing – especially at the LaSalle – Peru turnoff. A gas station or two and perhaps a small café. During the early '50's, it seemed that it occurred to a group that the area was the right place for development. Suddenly, one went to a boat race at Lake DePue and there were modern facilities out at 80 LaSalle-Peru interchange – there was a Holiday and gosh the Tiki complex.

Before getting to the Tiki, one must consider the Holiday Inn. That venerable institution had spring up over the US at likely places a traveler was likely to stop. It was not astounding that the chain located LaSalle, Highway 80.

If course, it became popular with the boat race crowd – it had a café, a lounge, a swimming pool and a banquet hall – all the amenities. It also had a bad management.

1956 Mt. Carmel Illinois NOA Alky Nationals

Left to Right: Paul Hayes, Stan Leavendusky, Alex Gomback.

A book could be written about the exploits of these three. Hayes owned a motel and café in the small town of Thayer, Missouri. He started boat racing as a driver, then became an "Angel" for a few talented drivers.

Leavendusky ever prominent in his farmers overalls was a giant talent in Alky boat racing. He was an absolutely first class boat driver and his engine building resulted in incredible success for himself, his son Jr and virtually everyone who has owned one of his PR, Konig, Mercury and Evinrude SC motors.

Gomback, a Cleveland sheet metal specialist was a tenacious outboard runabout driver during the early post war era.

The bad experiences were legion. A few may be mentioned. Stanley Leavendusky, Jr. sent a deposit check for a room, which was deposited. Jr. arrived at the desk and requested a room "Sorry we are full up and there is no room available. But I have a cancelled check" Result, no room and no return deposit.

Same thing happened to Marshal Grand. Different result. Grant was a personal friend of the Holiday Inn founder. He placed a phone call to the major-domo who says, "Give me ten minutes." He contacted the LaSalle manager and says, "Give Mr. Grant a room or I'll pull your franchise." Marshal got a room and whatever he wanted.

Other abused customers, perhaps in the spirit of exuberant fun, drove a car into the swimming pool. One could state other dynamic experiences but this is a tome of fun and games – not a black treatise.

About this time the Tiki Motel complex grew up. First, as a fuel stop for truckers then the Pine Cone Cafe & motel were added. The motel consisted of three buildings, the office and its adjoining room, the multi-story middle building and then the two story building alongside Highway 80.

The two outer buildings – smoking allowed – had a patina, a strange exotic aroma – a rich blend of tobacco and other scent that some folks thought unpleasant. The middle building was favored by the more seasoned travelers – no smoking and the odor seemed more pleasant.

There were some who did not favor the Tiki. One could not find fault with its moderate price and the extremely agreeable manager. She was a sweet old lady who remembered your name from year to year and was pleased to have you visit the week during each year. It was known the owner wanted to close the

Tiki long before doing so – but delayed because he could not bear to retire the lady who managed the complex.

Certainly there were many who did not favor the Tiki. This may seem curious to those who see those who put-up with a camping trip to Maine where the moose can be heard all night or a fishing trip where the mosquitos can frighten a bald eagle.

Prices in northwest Illinois during the '50's and '60's were quite low. The Pine Cone Café was a good example. The place was divided – part for truckers and the other for the general public – there was no segregation- the separation seemed automatic. The help was friendly. One could ask for cracked ice in the glass of milk – no problem.

A coffee pot was often placed on the breakfast table – help yourself. Should one want the chicken extra crispy – no problem.

The Pine Cone was more than a café for the boat race crowd – it was a congenial meeting forum. After the events of each day at Lake DePue, the tables were filled till late each night with the boat race crowd discussing their favorite topic – boat racing.

The Tiki and Pine Cone are no more. The hall of the Motel no longer sound with the tread of the giants of outboard boat racing or rasp with the Berlin accent of Hans Kraage or Dieter Konig; the rapid stattico of central Italy – G. Rossi' the sibilant sound of Hideo Kishimotor; the Australian lilt of John Hudson, Southern drawl of Ralph Donald.

Ralph Donald, Marietta, Georgia crosses the finish line as winner of a heat in 250 cc Alky Runabout at the APBA Pro (Alky) Nationals.

Donald, a real estate broker, began his outboard racing career in the early '50's and soon became a formidable competiror in the Pro runabout classes. Because of knee problems, he switched to hydroplanes and continued a career that carried into his '80's.

Ralph gave back to the sport in many ways. He was APBA race referee, Region Chairman, Pro (Alky) Commission Chairman and often represented the USA in European regattas. He was also the promoter who brought VIM World Championships to America.

1955 Florida

Dieter Konig, Berlin, Germany and his bride pose with a Swift hydro, while at a test site in Florida.

Dieter often came to the USA for it was his biggest sales market and he wanted to make sure America know the potential for his racing motors.

The business was started by his father prior WWII. Dieter took over and soon made a name for the brand by driving as a factory team member.

His American importer, Scott Smith, Dallas, Georgia, did a fine job in promoting the brand, Konig enjoyed his American experiences and wanted to help Smith in every way possible.

*****

2012 DePue IL APBA Alky Nationals

Duke Johnson – driver

This Johnson PR-65 powered hydro speed is about 68 mph. Not bad for a motor that was designed in 1934. The 13/19 lower unit gear ration does require a large propeller which will kick the boat around and does not allow a high rpm.

The APBA antique category is populated by owners and drivers who appreciate the old iron and have a huge amount of fun racing such equipment.

*Jack Corner, age 79, piloting his Class A Stock Runabout. The boat is in the middle of a turn –
note that the throttle is squeezed right.*

*Jack began his boat racing career shortly after WWII. During the war, he had been a pilot of a
B-24 and was on the first 1943 Polesti, Romania mission where 25% of aircraft did not return
to base in North Africa – A trip of over 2400 miles.*

*He built and designed his own boats. He specialized in the small stock racing classes, where he
established national speed competition records in the '50's. After retiring from a job as
national sales manager for a paint spray can manufacturer, he moved to Florida and at the
age of 75 resumed boat racing, driving an A Stock Runabout. Jack is no longer present but he
will be remembered as a fine competitor and innovator.*

The 20' DeSilva wing won the 9 hour event with a margin of only about 20-30 seconds.
*The #31 wing differed from the Switzer wing in that the Switzer was a tunnel hull with vented
sponsons, whereas the #31 had a single-step sponson. The Switzer was probably the most
technically pure design but #31 was specifically designed to compete under the conditions to
be encountered in a Marathon.*
*Water would be rough – there were over 100 boats entered – Inboard and Outboard. A fuel
tank of 40 gallons was placed in each sponson mid-ship of the aft-plane – the boat had to carry
a large weight, at speed.*
*Ron Hill drove a similar type boat but one without a wing. It had a typical sponson, which
tended to slide in turning. Ron was only slightly behind going into the last turn, but went into
the Buoy very fast – the boat slid wide and by the time he got around the turn, #31 had
smoothly rounded the buoy and received the checkered flag.*
*Jimbo McConnel and Frank Zorkin drove another DeSilva Wing – placed fifth (they had some
mechanical problems). Photo-Squires.*

1970 Outboards Gun Down Inboards at Parker (That was the headline by the June issue of Powerboat Magazine)

Photo shows Alan Stinson, Pittsburg, about to cross the finish line at the 9 hour marathon, in first place. His co-driver was Jerry Walin, Seattle.

This was the first combined race between inboards and outboard in which the outboard had been the victor. In fact, the win was so decisive that never again were the two camps were ever to engage. Inboard with their mighty auto engines could produce speed, but their drive train could not stand the abuse of many hours of destructive strain. In fact, the outcome was embarrassing – why add insult to injury by doing it again!?!?

There were 102 starters, 50 were inboards and 52 outboards. Stinson and Walin averaged 81mph for the 9 hours and last lap was timed at 97mph. Outboards took 9 of the first places, 18 of the first 20.

The Stinson/Walin boat was a 20' DeSilva step Tunnel design with a Clark Y center wing. The single step design was used – it was thought that a more rapid acceleration and punch was needed more that the theoretical speed advantage of the vented sponsor design of the Switzer Wing boat.

Although turning capability was not paramount careful consideration was given to that factor – we wanted the boat to lock-up in the turns. Sliding, with little control, is not good when 102 boats are competing in a limited amount of water.

Ron Hill, Los Angeles, in a twin Evinrude powered OMC boat finished a close second. Jimbo McConnel, Needles, and Frank Zorkin, Phoenix, placed 5th in another 20' DeSilva wing. They had bad luck, in that they spent 3 laps in the pits due to dead batteries.

2+2=4

Hold On! Hold On! Those ancient theorists are right. (You and I may agree) But what about modern scientists and intellectuals?

The following is a story that was going around when I was racing. "I have not heard it repeated for many years – you may have missed it."

A CEO of a large company was plagued with a lot of inventory, distribution, marketing and the economy…the usual.

He thought 2+2 still equal 4 or am I living in the past. He called in for a conference, his engineer, his lawyer and finally his accountant.

He asked his engineer to give him the answer to 2+2. Without hesitation the engineer says "2+2 equals 4, of course." Ok, the CEO thought, I'm on track, but I'd better get some more advice.

He asked his lawyer the same question. The lawyer thought for a moment and said, "Well 2+2 could mean 3-3/4,3-7/8 or 4-2/16,4-1/8 – it depends on the circumstance. Maybe even 4."

The CEO thought about that – was not entirely satisfied, so finally called in the accountant and asked the question. What is the answer to 2+2?

Louis Williams & Jim Shook

The accountant thought for a moment, pulled down the window shades, turned off the tape recorder, took the CEO over to the corner and asked, "What do you want it to mean?"

"This story probably goes back to the Romans. In fact, Pluto may have been the author. You were thinking E=MC2? Forget it, keep things simple.

Jim Shook – V5 and Louis Williams 14T are each trying to get to the turn first.

It looks like Williams, on the inside, has the advantage. However Shook was able to overtake 14T and place in their heat of 250cc (class Alky) runabout at the NOA, Lake Spivey regatta. They are both using Quincy Mercury motors, with open exhaust pipes.

The open exhaust mega-phones are seldom on modern racing motors today. The tuned expansion chamber pipes are much more efficient, with little offensive noise.

Photo-Rome

This and That

Competition in the early days of outboard racing was often a serious affair. And, as if often the case when things get serious, some drivers may do things that go beyond the pale.

One driver in 1930 found an evil way to beat the competition. He lived in Moss Landing, California, and was known to have a generous supply of granulated sugar that sometimes found itself in the gas tank of his competition. Sugar Sanchez was his nickname, not his legal name.

*****

Everyone likes Fred Miller. Everyone appreciates his contributions to the sport of boat racing. Over a long career he has been a race promoter, APBA office holder, Referee at race events, and very good outboard race boat driver.

We sold Fred a Stock division runabout some years ago. He was quite successful. Within a short time he won several National titles. Proof of his likeability was the fact that most of his championships were won with borrowed motors and propellers. A superior motor is a precious thing. A superior propeller is a very rare and important tool that must be treated accordingly. To loan this type of equipment is only done with great caution: Fred Miller used such parts over a very long period of time.

*****

It was mostly rolling hill country, 15 or 20 miles between small towns with perhaps just a gas station, general store and post office.

We had given ourselves enough time to get to Lake Village; we were in no hurry. The road was a paved two-lane, but traffic was light and the weather was clear.

We had stopped in Shreveport the night before. The motel had been recently built, a restaurant had provided an acceptable meal, so we entered Arkansas with good spirit.

We stopped for gas near mid-day. A young boy gave us good and friendly service. I asked, "Which way out of town, going Fast?" He replied, "I don't know, I've never been out of town!" A while later another village came up and we stopped for lunch.

We entered what looked like the only café in town.

The waitress asked, "Anything to drink?"

"Yes, ice tea."

"Fine, four ice tea! No menus, we have burgers, double burgers, cheese burgers, grits, Brunswick stew, barbecue, buckles and gravy, fries and chicken fried steak."

"Hmm- wait, this team is sweet, I didn't order sweet tea!"

"That's the way it comes: sweet."

"You don't have any unsweetened tea?"

"No, just sweet."

"I don't like sweet tea."

"Well, we have Coke. Maybe there's couple bottles of Dr. Pepper."

*****

Sam Hanks was an Indianapolis 500 winner. He lived in Southern California and enjoyed water sports.

He had operated a few fast boats. Some friends talked him into becoming a member of a quartet of drivers who were to race at a short Salton Sea outboard marathon. They were to drive a 17' Power Cat tunnel boat. The boat was similar in design to the 1920's Mullins which had a relatively narrow tunnel that ended in depth at the transom. The sponsons were rather narrow and quite flat.

The race was in progress when Sam began driving. After his allotted time, he got out of the boat and said, "You guys are crazy! That was the most awful gut-busting experience I've ever had, the boat did everything but go to the moon. I don't know how I stayed in there. Feels like I've been massaged by an elephant. This is supposed to be fun?"

1979 Lake Spivey Louisiana
Bill DeSilva, left, is telling Louis Williams, Beaumount, Texas how to maintain the integrity of his boat bottom.
"Digger" Williams, a mortician, was a veteran class A and B Alky runabout driver, who had started his racing career with Texas built boats. It took awhile before Louis entered the DeSilva brand. He was a consistent frontrun competitor, with a support group headed by Joe Rome.
Louis won several national championships but a noteworthy one was at Lake Acworth, Georgia in 1980. He was then near the end of his boat racing and a championship was a great way to end a career.

Photo-Rome

*****

The unique smell of Dynex racing fuel that permeated the pits of outboard racing in the '30's and '40's and '50's was so pervasive that one could often visit a workshop, garage or storeroom and find an open can of the fuel—just so that the area would be perfumed!

Bug Wiget, a chemical engineer graduate of Cal-Tech in Pasadena, California, once said, "The smell of Dynex was due to the inclusion of various higher alcohols that were by-products of fractioning columns at DuPont's ammonia plant in Wilmington, Deleware. Probably Octyl alcohol and related alcohols of around C/8 range. Dynax was patented."

*****

Rpm x Pitch x .095 / Gear ratio =speed.

This is the speed formula one can use to determine why desired speed is not attained.

*****

A universal law: change is fought by all who stand to lose, as well as by those who stand to gain, simply because they are afraid of changing.

*****

Daniel Bernoulli: mathematician and Scientist, burn in 1700 in Groningen, Netherlands, died in 1782 in Basel, Switzerland.

His law of hydro-dynamics: Pressure is inversely proportional to speed.

*****

Isaac Newton: Physicist - mathematician, born in 1642 in Lincolnshire, England, died in 1727 in Middlesex.

Newton's Laws of Motion:

1.   A body at rest tends to stay at rest.
2.   A body in motion tends to remain in motion.

3. When a first body exerts force on a second body, the second body exerts simulations force on the first body.

Newton's momentum Theorem:

The force exerted by the fluid on the body is equal to the rate of change in momentum in the fluid due to the presence of the body.

The body moving through the medium experiences impacts from all the particles in its path and consequently imparts momentum to them. The total mass of all the particles impacting the body per second is pAw. This mass is given a velocity W, which is proportional to the velocity W of the body.

$D = pAww' = fApw2$

[D=drag, W=Velocity, P=Density of Fluid, A=Area of body in direction of flow; f=Factor of proportionality]

*****

January 1989 Dallas Georgia

Bill DeSilva, Stan McDonald, Ralph DeSilva

McDonald – renown Canadian outboard race engine builder.

Photo-Williams

This runabout is the last boat built of the Delta design.

A combination of a basic runabout with elements of a tunnel (Catamaran), the Delta series was designed to cope with problems encountered by a basic runabout competing at high speed,

The design is not legal in the US. However, the boat is acceptable in Australia and has a home in Sidney.

Sometime in the future the runabout will be accepted as the superior high speed boat in contrast to the step hydro – as a competition vehicle.

Then, the Delta design concept may be accepted as a good competition addendum to the basic runabout.

John Hudson, Sydney, Australia drives the DeSilva design small tunnel hull with which he set a National Kilo record of 102.8 kph in 1988, then another mark of 63.47 mph, 550c Super Sport (yamato model 102, 27 March 1989).

A profile of John Hudson can be found in his bibliographical article. Boat racing in Australia did not follow the course set in the US. Their sport was not a structure activity which evolved over time. It was a loose federation of groups and individuals that were largely doing their own thing in a congregation of boats and imported motors – some sophisticated but most raced out of the box.

Their inboard boat racing has been dominated; the outboards are a side show. The country is huge, the population is sparse. Availability of water is critical to any society and in Australia the water supply has always been a matter of political and social concern. The ocean is the only source that be used with impunity and the ocean is not a venue for small boats of high speed.

John Hudson

In March 2013 my good American friend, Ralph DeSilva, asked if I would contribute an article to his autobiography. I am happy to do this as I am one of Ralph's friends who have been urging him to document his life story. Ralph's daughter, Ann, has also been keen for suggestion and I am to add an Australian flavor to this piece, covering our friendship, the country in general, the political system, boat racing, and in his words, "Whatever else." Some task! So, I hope this article is on track and adds to his full and long life story.

My first correspondence with Ralph and his younger brother Bill was in 1973, seeking their advice on race boat designs. I was 26, and I calculated that Ralph was about 51 and Bill 47. Now Ralph is aged 90, and I am almost 67. Unfortunately Bill passed away in 1998 at the age of 72. We all know Bill was Ralph's best friend. To bill's wife Betty and Ralph, this was a very sad occasion. We all miss Bill DeSilva.

In February 1976 a boat racing friend and I travelled to America to attend the Parker 9 hour Enduro. We stopped in San Francisco and met Ralph and Bill. They took us to breakfast and generally entertained us for most of a day. The usual digs at Aussies for excessive consumption of alcohol and Kangaroos in the center of Sidney were handled well by us neither of us being drinkers. We also scored some points on Americans. The banter was lively. We all had a good time, and at the end I think the score was nil all; well not really, because Bill DeSilva scored the winning try. Australians use their knife and fork differently to Americans. We are more in the English way. Bill's last observation won the debate when he matter-of-factly said to Ralph, "...and they eat funny too Ralph." From that

Lake Glenmaggie, Victoria.

This is how a lake looked in Australia in 1985. John Hudson, Sidney, has just looped his boat while making a kilo attempt. The young boat driver was able at a later date to successfully establish several national (and world) records for small OPC Type Deep V runabouts and tunnels.

first meeting a strong and long-lasting friendship developed between me and the DeSilva's. It is now over 40 years since our first encounter, and we are still going strong, God willing.

The DeSilva's were based in Sebastopol, CA, operation out of an old barn and building mainly alky runabouts. Some tunnel hulls were also produced, along with hydro's. They were reluctant to supply race boat plans. Little did I know at the time that I was about the only person to whom they would supply plans of their race boats.

In 1977 Ralph, Bill and I attended the Stock Outboard Nationals in Bakersfield, CA. At this venue I first saw Yamato Model 80 racing outboard motors. The American agent at that time was Japanese/American Tommy Ige. Tommy later retired to Hawaii. Then in 1980 we went to St. Paul, MI for the Alky Nationals. These races were cancelled due to the high rate of flow in the Mississippi. From there we drove to Atlanta with real estate agent and boat racer Ralph Donald. By then Ralph, Bill and Betty and their young children, Marie and Patrick, had decided to relocated to the South. May of their customers would be closer at hand, and I think they believed life would be a little bit easier down south. They purchased land in Dallas, GA and I helped them peg out the new factory site. They built a custom designed building, new for the first time in their careers. Betty and Bill purchased a lovely large house on a large area of land.

The in 1984 I took my wife Debbie and our one year old son Robert to visit the DeSilvas in Georgia. We were made welcome at Betty's and Bill's new home and were general treated to a wonderful time. A car was even provided for our use. One couldn't ask for better hospitality. The occasion was the Alky outboard Nationals at Acworth, not far from the DeSilva's home. There we met Bill and Ralph's mother. Betty and Bill spend most of a day with us at the Civil War Museum. What a terrible time in your history, but I believe it ultimately contributed to the building of a stronger and greater nation. We visited Stone Mountain, I went to the top with a friend whil Debbie, Robert, Betty and Bill stayed below and rode the train. In Australia's Northern territory we have a massive monolith called Ayers Rock (Aboriginal Name 'Uluru'), worth visiting if travelling down under. One night Ralph shouted Debbie and me to a meal out while Betty and Bill minded young Robert. This was the first time we had left our first son to be minded. Debbie was keen to get back. Thanks Betty and Bill for our free night out. Robert is now 29 and the father of a 10 month old Alya Nicole Hudson. The flights were long (24 hours each way), but the memories are great.

Twenty years and five more children later I took my 19 year old second ton, Ben to meet Ralph in Atlanta. This was 2004, and the three of us drove from Atlanta to DePue IL. I Met Ralph's good friend John Herberg on this trip. John and I are souls mates in collecting old outboard motors, me, Scott and John mostly OMC. We all had a terrific time campaigning Tim Webber's equipment. This was the first time I met Ralph's daughter Ann, a wonderful and charming lady. I also became friends with Bernie Van

Osdale. Bernie has written and published a very good book on the history of American power boat racing, and is a racer in the Antique Classes driving a DeSilva runabout.

Four years later (2008) I travelled back to the US, driving with Ann and Ralph to DePue, where we raced with antiques again. From there I was handed over to the Herbergs, and John, Merrilene and I drove to Tomahawk for the Antique Outboard motor Club (AOMCI) Nationals. I brought home about 25 old Scotts and a restorable 1962 15ft Scott boat. The Herbergs owned Moline Boat and Motor which is run these days by their son Bob. We swap motors, Australiana and items of American culture. Bob Herberg has a large kangaroo hazard picture road sign on his garage door.

In 2010 I repeated the previous trip. I collected more 'treasures'.

The above is a necessarily abbreviated account of my times while being in Ralph's company. But there is more. In 1984 I purchased two Yamato Model 102 racing motors from the then American dealer, Jim McKean. Jim passed away recently. Back home I approached our APBA with a view to start a one motor stock outboard class in Australia. The class was to be based on the Yamato 102 motor and later motors that follow it. The class was established. We now race 102, 202, 202SL, and 302 Yamato motors in the class. Ralph and Bill DeSilva embraced the Australian class and provided me with plans for a small (10'6") tunnel hull. We built five of these boats ourselves, and others were constructed off Ralph's plans. Although all types of hull design are legal in the class, it is the DeSilva Tunnel that was, and is still, dominant. Ralph refused to take a royalty on the boats built. With the DeSilva's help we had a unique boat that was the envy of Yamato outboard racers the world over. Ralph's little boat could handle choppy water better than a runabout or hydro, and was capable of well over 60 mph even with our regulation two blade Yamato bronze propeller. Recognition was such that we had a request from Yamato Motor Company in Japan for a boat. We shipped a very successful hull to them. Their chief driver then proceeded to blow it over backwards right in front of the company President and his staff. I swapped the boat for two motors, but I think the Japanese went cold on the tunnel hull idea! I was concerned that the hull would be copied in Japan. I ran this past Ralph, but he said he was not concerned about that eventuality. I thought that he was generous in his attitude. Later on we shipped another hull to Saipan.

Ralph and Bill built a 13'6" tunnel hull for me in about 1978. This boat was powered by a stock 3 cylinder 75hp short-shaft Evinrude. TO this day no Evinrude/Johnson stinger has Kiloed faster. We went through the kilo averaging 82.145 mph. In a four lap sprint race I could hold off 15' monos powered by 150XC Mercs for two of the four laps. Ultimately the bigger motors (twice the capacity and power) had more torque and could out accelerate the tunnel from corners. But the DeSilva was faster. Then in 1994 Ralph and Bill build out sons, Robert and Ben, a small racing runabout. It was a gift from Ralph and Bill. The two boys used it in our junior classes. It is a great design, and I now intend to rig it with an old Yamato 102, and go racing. At my age it will be fast enough.

I think Ralph is responsible for me becoming an avid reader. When I was a teenager, and into my twenties, my parents did their best to interest me in reading. I did always read novels and magazines, but not as regularly as I do now. I the early 1990's Ralph started to regularly send out books. We now are kindred spirits in devouring novels by the likes of Tom Clancy, Lious L'Amour, Tony Hillerman, Neville Shute, and many more. I think I have every Louis L'Amour book! I am now an avid reader generally. Thank you Ralph.

Over the years Ralph and Bill sent our kids many presents, basket balls, caps and video. Much appreciated.

Boat racing "Down Under" is of the two usual types, outboard and inboard. The perception is that "real Aussie blokes" generally race V8's. But, some "real Aussie blokes" do race outboards. Just joking, but I do not wish to alter the stereotypes of us Aussies. These days our governing body is the "AUSTRALIAN POWER BOAT ASSOCIATION". All the States have their APBA's and these are affiliated with the National body. From rule books, the National APBA web site, and my own knowledge I have garnered the following information. As well as racing I tried to do my duty as a club official. My roles have been 6 years Federal APBA Secretary, 12 years NSW state APBA Treasurer, an Australian Referee since 1985, and Club Delegate to our NSE APBA for some years in the 80's and 90's. I have not been active as a referee since the middle 1990's.

The first recorded race too place on July 6th 1905 at the "Motor Boat Club" in Sydney, probably at Rose Bay in Sydney Harbor. Then on 29 November, 1929 the "Power Boat Association of Australia" was incorporated and held races in the harbor. States represented were NSW, Queensland, and Victoria all on the eastern seaboard. (Austaliasia takes in Australia, New Zealand, and Papua/New Guinea). Between club racing there were major events conducted. The first Australian Championship in 1909, and in 1912 Griffith Cop Unlimited Championship. By 1927 outboards were popular contenders and the O'Donoghue Shield became the unlimited outboard trophy. It still is today. The first, 1927, outboard event was held at the Royal Motor Yacht Club, Rose Bay. Mr. E.A. Williams was victorious in 'ELTO'. To me this is proof that early Evinrude and Johnson quad racing motors were raced in Australia. Indeed, I have located two of these motors and sent them to collector John Herberg in Carbon Cliff, IL.

In March, 1933, our NSW APBA formed and affiliated with the Federal APBA. WW2 prevented major races from 1939 to 1944. From July, 1955, all of the Australian states had formed their organizations and joined the overall governing body as affiliates. The scene was then set for state to state, and federal rivalry, which has continued in both constructive and destructive times to the present day. Overall the structure has worked well for the sport.

Most inboards are big engine V8 boats, in various classes. Outboards run the full gambit from junior classes, through mid-horsepower, to various classes of V6 powered tunnels. Over time the outboard have been declining in numbers relative to inboard classes, although of late I have noticed the outboard growing again. Yamato and 25hp racing are the entry level outboard classes after junior classes. I feel there is a gradual decline in our sport in comparison to the total of outdoor activities in Australia. This can in part be explained by increasing costs and complexity involved with safety (both boat and venue), the suburban sprawl and noise regulations. The cost of insurance (especially after 9/11) are causing the small events to flounder, giving ruse to larger spectacular events. And there are necessarily fewer of these. When I started racing in the late 1960's a driver had a boat, a club, and you raced. It's a lot more complicated now. I did not play computer games indoor as a kid, either. Motor sports generally are still strong in Australia, but their character has changed. I think it's an unavoidablc sign of the times. My club was Sydney Outboard Club. It folded in 2002. Victoria had the Victorian Outboard Racing Club and the Victorian Outboard Club, both gone. The Prop Riders Club in Queensland is still operating. Sydney now has three strong clubs left. These being Upper Hawkesbury Power Boat Club, Deepwater PBC, and St. George Motor Boat Club. I now belong to UHPBC. It is a strong and active club for outboards and inboards. There are many active clubs in regional areas that cater to racing and other water sports.

When I started racing in the 1960's boat racing was well delineated between outboard and inboard lines. I came in on the trail end of outboard and inboard lines. I came in on the tail end of outboard hydroplanes racing. There was still outboard hydroplane racing, but the trend was towards recreational motors powering plywood or fiberglass monos. What American racers call "Commercial" motors we call "Stock". My thinking is that we swung more to racing commercial motors and classes because about this time large American outboard brands were becoming readily available and affordable in Australia. Scott outboards in 40hp and 60hp were here. Johnson/Evinrude motors were being built at Bankstown, Sydney. And Mercury motors were assembled in Melbourne.

So our outboard classes were then heavily skewed toward racing these motors at the expense of our older pure hydro and runabout classes. The only USA oriented stock class racing here now is our Yamato class (OSY400A). In the 1970's I did race a McCulloch 630 powered hydro, but my main emphasis was with an 11'6" V bottom Haines Hunter Spyder powered with a Short shaft Merc 50. Today there are still outboard hydro classed listed (C,D, F Unlimited) but, with a few exceptions, not many "Stock" or Alky motor races. Main classes were 25hp, 45ci, 61ci, 75ci, 100ci, and unlimited. These classes were split into "Family" and "Sports". Family class was monos, a passenger and 1.5 in maximum cavitation plate height. Sports class dropped all restrictions and hulls could be tunnels. Common sense saw the passenger removed from the family class rules, on safety grounds, in the late seventies. I raced a DeSilva Hydro with a 25SS Mercury in the 1970's. But this was against hulls of any configuration in our 5500cc Super Sport Class. I would still like to race a low powered hydro.

One Australian Hydro racer who I met in the late 1970's regularly raced in the US. Jack Marshall, and wife Di, divided their time between the US and Australia. The Marshalls had a house in Knoxville and one in Sydney. Summers in both countries, now that's a good life! Jack raced Konig powered hydros in the US racing season and I remember him at our National Championships racing the same rigs. The Marshalls were good friends of Art Pugh and his wife, also from Knoxville. I remember that Debbie and I were dinner guests of the Marshalls at their Maroubra home in about 1978. The house was two stories, with the whole ground floor given over to machine tools. He was innovative, and at one stage raced a motor with two Konig power heads side by side driving a single midsection and propeller. I lost track of Jack, but found out that they moved to Queensland's Gold Coast in retirement. Jack passed away recently. Ralph and bill knew Jack Marshall and often asked me about him.

Today the classes are in metric. We have junior (6hp and 15hp), 25hp, OSY400A (Yamato), 550cc, 800cc, 1000cc, 1250cc 2000cc, 2.4ltr and UIM F1. These are circuit racing and some are mono as well as tunnel. Outboards also have offshore and drag representation.

The inboard classes cover Displacement Hull, Hydroplane, and Offshore. Motor sizes range from 1.5ltr to unlimited capacity supercharged. Displacement hulls are defined as non-tunnel or hydro. Most large engine boats are "V" drive, while the tunnels are I/O driven. In Australia the Ford or Chevy V8 is the preferred power plant, and most are highly and expensively modified. Some large hydros run Rolls Royce Merlin engines and aircraft jets. There is serious competition between New Zealand and Australia for the unlimited Griffith Cup. The winner takes it home, in the next year the race takes place in his country. Very serious NZ/Aussie rivalry. Outboards are eligible, but would be totally outpaced by the unlimited hydros.

Australian drivers have been awarded 369 100mph badges, and 33 200kph badges. And Australia still holds the World Water Speed Record at 317.6mph. Ken Warbly established this speed in "Spirit of Australia" on October 8, 1978 at Blowering dam, in the NSW Snowy Mountains. His previous World Record was 289.9mph, set march 13 1976. This body of water is a large man-made reservoir. It was part of the hydroelectric complex that delivers back-up energy to Sydney and Melbourne in peak load times. Ken Warbly's speed record will probably stand for many years. General opinion is that his speed and anything higher is extremely dangerous. For almost 30 years there have been suggestions of attempts, but nothing has eventuated. It was brave and pretty damn fast!

*****

Now to the Country of Australia. (The Great Southern Land). A (Very) Short history.

Our landmass area is roughly that of the continental United States. If you turn one or the other map upside down they are a close match. We are a very old continent and the talent mountain, Mt. Kosciuszko, is 7,310 ft high. This is a measure of geological time and weathering. Captain James Cook discovered the east coast in HMS Endeavour in 1770. The penal settlement was established with the First Fleet in January 25,1788. The youngest convict was John Hudson, my namesake, aged, 9 years, a chimney sweep and orphan. He was transported for breaking and entering. Hudson was sentenced to 8 years transportation to the American colonies in 1783, but after that avenue ended found himself on the First Fleet landing in NSW in 1788. We are now over 24 million in population, with 25% of the people being born outside Australia! We are high-tech and a small, but influential player on the world stage. Of late much of our industry has been depleted by cheaper manufacturers of Asia, China especially. Australia is very rich in minerals and agriculture and is a large supplier to the world. I do worry about the future. There is an American connection to the early colony in Sydney Cove. In 1790 the colony was experiencing starvation because the English had great trouble growing crops in the sandy soil that abounds around the early settlement site, and a year after first landing the colony was running out of food and starving. As the story goes an American ship arrived loaded with food and Rum. The skipper refused to sell the food until all the rum was sold off at very profitable prices. As the colonial government had no money the convict guards pooled their resources and bought all the rum, then sold it to the convicts and free settlers at a big profit margin. Rum became the alternate currency in NSW and was heavily traded. From that day the nick name of the NSW Police Force has been "The Rum Corps". Time has seen this moniker worn with honor. It is believed that James Cook's Endeavor ended her days burnt and sunk to block the entrance to Boston during the American War of Independence. The US government has returned parts of her to Australia.

We are a parliamentary Constitutional Monarchy, with a Westminster style government, steeped in the traditions of Magna Carta. The Queen is nominally Head of State, though the Governor General, but the reality is such that we are a totally independent nation. There have been referenda in the past to totally break free from Britain. All have failed. The Two main reasons being that: 1. You cannot trust politicians to come up with a system that worked better and 2: "If it ain't broke, don't fix it". We have six states and one large territory on this island continent. I regret to tell the citizens of America that five of these are "Bigger than Texas" in area. The Federal parliament has an upper and lower house, this lower house is the house of representatives and is where all the action happens. Our two main partys are very similar in philosophy to their American counterparts. The Liberal party (republicans) and the labor party (conservatives). Similar in philosophy but not identical. Each state has its own parliament. As in the federal sphere the government and leader belong to the majority party. The state leader is the "premiere". The NSW lower house is generally considered to be the toughest in the western world, knick-named "The Blood House." Although the Queen is technically Head of State, the reality is such that the PM advises Her Majesty of the Government decisions. The Queen's representative then agrees with government policy. Hence no need to change the system.

Australia is a major ally of the United States. We fight together, and unfortunately, die together. Both counties are very close in ideology, character, and norms and freedoms. An example of this is that our youngest son, Andrew (23), has just spent seven months as a soldier in Afghanistan. He came home safe, but not all his friends did.

And now to the weather. It's generally terrific. Hot in summer, Cold in winter, but not the extremes of Northern America. We have a good snow field which attract many northern hemisphere dwellers because our seasons are opposite. In the Red Centre it is mostly dry, but when it rains it really rains, and floods. Our young people swim, surf, play sports and computer games: not necessarily in that order.

These clippings (above and next page) are from an Australian Magazine, the Yamato-tunnel class is still ongoing today. John Hudson has written an essay on Australian Boat Racing— past and present.

John Hudson's article Now to the Country of Australia. (The Great Southern Land). A (Very) Short history. is included above.

the Yamato story

Rodney Lawsons recently gave me a test drive of his record holding Yamato tunnel boat called *Lawsons Video Services*. I met him early on Saturday morning at the Sydney Outboard Club on the upper Georges River in Sydney.

The main purpose was to check the hull out and to get some photos, but it seemed that once the boat was in the water it was near impossible to get Rodney out of it again. The nine foot hull hurled up and down the Georges River at 60 M/ph for about an hour, barely using any fuel (these boats do the Bridge to Bridge on 20 litres). There were none of the mechanical problems associated with some race boats. That was enough — I wanted a drive.

I found myself kneeling in this tiny hull with a motor screaming at 7000rpm. They take a while to get on the plane, but the moment the props grip the water you experience rapid acceleration to 50 M/ph plus, and that's when the fun starts. These machines are extremely precise compared with conventional boats. The wing steering is super responsive and the hand throttle design gives you heaps of control. Kneeling in the boat may look strange, but once you're driving the boat it feels quite natural; sitting just would not provide the control over weight distribution that is required by this sort of race boat.

The message when cornering these tunnel hulls is don't slow down, because the hulls corner better at high speed. Low speed turns produce a very eerie feeling as the hull leans in the opposite direction to conventional hulls. The trick was to rapidly decelerate coming into the corner, and then flick it around the turn and immediately floor it back into the straight. After trying this a couple of times I discovered why tunnels always win in the corners.

On the straight the boat was brilliant with handling that defies the meaning of "nine foot boat". These tiny De Silva hulls handle the rough like a much larger

hull would, due to the very low centre of gravity. Speed is exaggerated because you're so close to the water — 60 M/ph feels like 80 M/ph.

The performance of this tiny race boat was brilliant, but the cost of getting into the class is a lot less than you would expect for this kind of exhilaration. I got some rough estimates from John Hudson as to the cost of setting up a hull, but it all really depends on how far you want to go. If you want to start with a simple hull (mono) and a reconditioned Yamato 102 motor, you can find yourself racing for less than $3000. Alternatively, if you want a near new rig the motor will cost $2100, including prop and wing steering, and a bare hull will cost between $500 and $2500, depending on whether you build one yourself from the De Silva plan, or get one built.

It's worth noting that all of the Yamato motors in Australia come in used and reconditioned after having a short life on the Japanese Paramutual Betting Circuit. It is for this reason that $3000 to $5500 will get you racing a boat that provides lots of excitement and has very low on-going running costs.

Next time you're at a race meeting and you're waiting around for the tiny mosquito powered boats to finish their race, remember two things — the drivers are having a great time out there, and there are 33 billion international dollars proving that big things happen in little packages.

If you want to find out more about Yamatos and the circuit, contact John Keevers on (045) 72 6202. □

John Hudson — the proud owner.

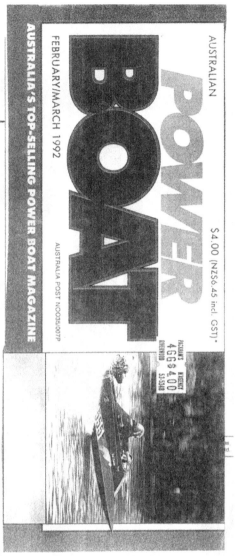

AUSTRALIA'S TOP-SELLING POWER BOAT MAGAZINE

FEBRUARY/MARCH 1992

AUSTRALIA POST NOO36/007P

AUSTRALIAN

$4.00 (NZ$6.45 incl. GST)*

POWER BOAT

RECORDS

Rodney Lawson: 1990-550 super sports — Bridge to Bridge in 67 minutes
"Sixty seven miles in sixty seven minutes"

John Keevers/John Hudson: National Kilo record holder — 550 super sports running 63.47 M/ph

Gary Thorn: Stock Yamato record: 61.9 M/ph

Left- 1961 John Toprahanian

John could get more out of 4:60 motor than anyone.

He built them for midget race cars for race boats and for fun., He was a bachelor, who could spend countless hours in his shop. John was a self-taught expert machinist – and he had all the tools.

One of his pet projects was working on and driving his re-built to new condition model T Ford Roadster.

Left- Driver- Charles Bailey Rider – Alan Ishii, California

Charles had purchased a recently introduced KR Alky runabout prior to the Winona Nationals. He had everything dialed-in for the race – he established a new competition record in one heat of the C Runabout (500cc) – had placed second to Bruce Nicholson, Texas, who had won the

championship. The two had identical equipment – the winner was essentially who got the better start.

Alana Ishii was small in stature, but large in talent as a driver. For that reason he was often asked to ride in the F runabout class. In the photo, it looks like he is ready to bail-out; but, we are assured it was merely the cause of a bouncing boat and no handles. Often a set of security handles were not installed in a cockpit and it was difficult for a rider to secure himself in a dynamic, bounding boat.

In this heat, the motor's lower unit broke and the outfit was unable to finish- for which Alan was grateful – "I had nothing to hang onto, everything was wet and slipper and I was all over the cockpit trying to stay aboard and not hamper Charlie."

1975 Winona Minnesota

Epilogue

The DeSilva boat company got its fifteen minutes of fame (actually 1-1/2 minutes) when a CBS reporter, over a National broadcast, asked Dick Pond who had built the hydro which he had just raced to win the NOA National Championship for class B hydro. Dick patted the boat and replied, "The boat was built by the DeSilva brothers of Los Angeles, California." The venue was on the Mississippi River in St. Paul, Minnesota, 1961.

1959 St. Paul

Bill DeSilva is front of two outboard racing legends – Dick Pond (Left) and Jerry Simison.

In 1959, Pond and Simison were barely out of their teens, but well on their way to becoming giants in the sport.

Pond could drive both hydro and runabout equally well. St. Paul, being on the rough Mississippi River, proved to be no obstacle to Pond, he won B (350c) Hydro in

dramatic fashion (Story elsewhere) and also dominated an outstanding field of D runabouts.

Jerry, son of a prominent physician, preferred the runabout. At St. Paul, he was not able to show ability due to motor problem.

*****

Oh, I've been on the sawdust trail for many a year

And I've had many a fear,

But, on the whole, it's been a lot of cheer.

I've met good and bad, but on a balance mostly solid folk,

Who knew how to cope.

From left to right: Lon Stevens

Ralph DeSilva

Lon Stevens was not a big man, in stature, but he had a giant reputation in outboard racing.

He started in a small way in 1954. He purchased a 13' runabout and a PR Johnson. At the time he was a teamster living in the San Francisco bay area. In 1956, he had progressed enough in driving ability to win a C class at the Long Beach APBA Nationals. This was a real accomplishment for his competition was all the Sport's best.

He then turned himself into a machinist-welder and began a career as an outboard race motor specialist. He became a highly efficient motor man and spent the rest of his life working on motors; driving them and helping his son John become a fine boat driver.

In 1960, he set a new C Service hydro kilo record of 61+ mph. Tom newton watched the run and said, "lon looks like you have a motor as good as mine." Lon built many C Service motors, but his real love was the four and six

2005 De Pue Illinois

■■■

Lon is quietly giving his formula for the perfect Martini. Ian Fleming may have been right – but did .007 have the formula!!!??
Had FDR known this perfect formula; the world today possibly would be different!!!

WESTERN UNION
TELEGRAM
W. P. MARSHALL, PRESIDENT
1201

LA157 AA196

A LDA133 PD=LAKELAND FLO 14 1130A EST=1962 MAY 14 AM 11 31

DE SILVA BOATS=

3215 SOUTH LA CIENEGA AVE CULVER CITY CALIF=

=SCRATCH FROM RECORD BOOK OLD STRAIGHTAWAY RECORDS IN
C RACING RUNABOUT. MY NEW RECORD 69.798 MADE AT FT
LAUDERDALE FLA MAY 12 USING DE SILVA SUPER C AND KONIG
MOTOR. CONGRATULATIONS ON THE LATEST OF A LONG LINE
OF RECORD BREAKING BOATS=

BUD WIGET==

C 69.798 12 C KONIG

THE COMPANY WILL APPRECIATE SUGGESTION FROM ITS PATRONS CONCERNING ITS SERVICE

WESTERN UNION
TELEGRAM
W. P. MARSHALL, PRESIDENT
1201

LA042 OB339 CTA114 SSA347

CT KVA064 NL PD=KNOXVILLE TENN 26=

B SILVA BOATS=   1959 APR 26 PM 1 3

3215 SOUTH LA CIENGA AVE CULVER CITY CALIF=

CHARLES HESTON SET FOR NOA WORLD RECORD HERE TODAY WITH
BRITISH ANZANI MOTORS, 73.620 MPH A HYRDO, 68.702 MPH
IN B RUNABOUT, 75.630 MPH IN B HYDRO AND 63.269 MPH IN
A RUNABOUT D EE SILVA BOATS USED FOR RUNABOUT RECORD IN
A HYDRO HE RAN 75 MPH ONE WAY AND IN B HYDRO 78 MILES
MPH ONE WAY=

BILL TENNY==

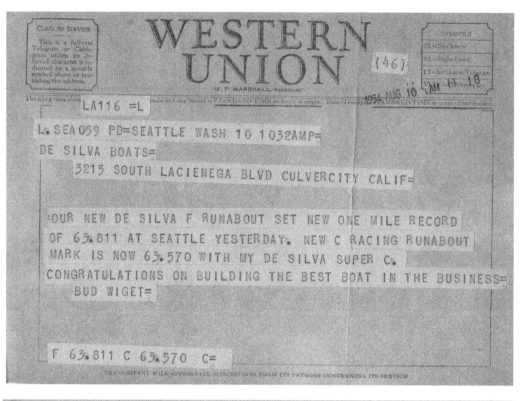

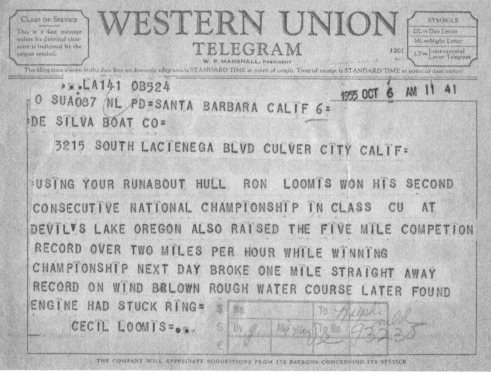

Index

BOAT RACING

THEN AND NOW

The topic of boat racing in America, which began (in a formal way) during the early 1920's is one replete with interesting facts, individual heroics and filled with technical development.

Then and Now provides a lively account of this activity on water. Boat racing took place wherever there was enough water to float a boat and a shoreline for spectators.

A race boat builder writes about those bitten by the bug of boat racing. Here are the famous and rich and middle class, the rare talent that always dominates in any endeavor and the everyday competitor who just wants to have a little gun and excitement.

Order Form

Please print names and address legibly.

Number of copies _____ ($_____)cash/check

Shipping:_____

Total:_____

Ship to address:

Name:_____

Address:_____

City/State:_____

Zip Code: _____

Phone: _____

Clip and send this form and payment to:

Ralph DeSilva
P.O. Box 1296
Hiram, GA 30132

Please include return address on the outside envelope.

CPSIA information can be obtained at www.ICGtesting.com
Printed in the USA
BVOW10s1921260615

406224BV00012B/57/P